Propaganda on Film
A Nation at War

Hayden Film Attitudes and Issues Series
RICHARD A. MAYNARD, Series Editor

Propaganda on Film
A Nation at War

RICHARD A. MAYNARD

Films Editor and Educational Film Reviewer
Scholastic Teacher Magazine

Formerly, Teacher of Social Studies and Afro-American History
Simon Gratz High School, Philadelphia; Community College of
Philadelphia; Great Lakes Colleges Association, Philadelphia

HAYDEN BOOK COMPANY, INC.
Rochelle Park, New Jersey

Library of Congress Cataloging in Publication Data
Main entry under title:

Propaganda on film.

   (Hayden film attitudes and issues series)
   Filmography: p.
   SUMMARY: An anthology exploring the relationship of
commercial films and political propaganda, particularly
concerning hot and cold wars.
   1.   Moving-pictures — Political aspects.   2.   Moving-
pictures in propaganda.   [1.   Motion pictures — Political
aspects.   2.   Motion pictures in propaganda]   I.   Maynard,
Richard A.
PN1995.9.P6P76   791.43′0909′35   75-6788
ISBN 0-8104-5897-7

1	2	3	4	5	6	7	8	9	PRINTING

75	76	77	78	79	80	81	82	83	YEAR

Editor's Introduction

May the shining flame of our enthusiasm never be extinguished. This flame alone gives light and warmth to the creative art of propaganda. Rising from the depths of the people, this art must always descend back to it and find its power there. Power based on guns may be a good thing; it is, however, better and more gratifying to win the heart of a people and to keep it.

Joseph Goebbels, Minister of Propaganda, Nazi Germany, 1934.

We can, by propaganda, widen the horizons of the schoolroom and give every individual . . . a living conception of the community which he has the privilege to serve. We can take his imagination beyond the boundaries of his community to discover the destiny of his country. We can light up his life with a sense of active citizenship. We can give him a sense of greater reality in the present and a vision of the future. And, so doing, we can make the life of the citizen more ardent and satisfactory to himself.

John Grierson, Director of the National Film Board of Canada, 1942.

. . . film and propaganda *had* to meet. Cinema is reality sifted, pointed and intensified; propaganda is a sifted, pointed, intensified idea used for a specific purpose. And their cooperation was a genuinely mutual one. First involuntarily, then more and more consciously, they have always leaned on each other. When cinema first became aware of its own language and power, it was, in fact, through propaganda. From then on, its great moments were also those of the "art of persuasion."

Robert Vas, British film critic and historian, 1963.

Propaganda—the persuasive dissemination of a particular set of attitudes and ideas to large masses of people—has been a political tool throughout the history of mankind. The political oratory of the ancient civilizations and the vast, forceful rhetoric accompanying Christian and Muslim missionaries were among the earliest examples of societal efforts at mass persuasion. With the invention of the printing press and the transportation revolution, mass media were developed, and propaganda became more extensive and more thorough. Governments in need of societal participation and support could draw on the power of the mass media to rally the citizens' spirit of patriotism. Indeed, there is probably no society in the world today which doesn't take some advantage of the vast potential of modern propaganda.

The term "propaganda" is a neutral one. It is, by itself, neither good nor bad, moral nor immoral, justifiable nor reprehensible. Since all modern societies use some form of mass persuasion—from patriotic campaigning, to mass education to commercial advertising—the key to evaluating its impact is in examining the framework in which it is used. In a particular society, are there situations in which some form of propaganda is absolutely necessary for its basic survival? Are there, or should there be, limits on the extent to which the techniques of mass persuasion can be used? Do the mass media make propaganda potentially exploitative and dangerous?

This anthology is designed to explore many of the issues concerning the uses of modern propaganda. It is composed of writings on the historical relationship between motion pictures and political propaganda. The writings trace the history of film as a mass persuasion medium, demonstrating how totalitarian societies (Soviet Russia and Nazi Germany) made use of it, and comparing this use to film propaganda in American democracy. The various sections of the anthology are composed of personal writings of film-maker-propagandists, essays by social and cinematic critics, contemporary film reviews, and screenplay extracts. They are designed to provide a broad base of examples of the uses and impact of film propaganda. Although the anthology concludes its analysis with the films of the middle-1950s (the so-called "McCarthyist" era), the implications of the principles of propaganda go beyond any arbitrary ending. With the impact of television as an extension of the film medium, many of the principles discussed in this unit can be applied to the status of today's mass propaganda. Indeed, after concluding this unit, all of the different kinds of film and television propaganda currently saturating our society should be examined. How do they resemble the various mass persuasion films of the past? Are today's products more sophisticated; more subtle? Have our propagandists learned any important lessons from the experience of the past? Has all of the criticism of the Griersons, the Agees, and the Warshows of potentially dangerous manipulation of public opinion through motion pictures been heeded by today's propagandists? It is the goal of this text to provoke this kind of analysis.

Extracts from several of the key films discussed in this unit are available from Films Incorporated in Wilmette, Illinois, on a 30-minute, 16-mm sound film, *Propaganda on Film: A Nation at War.*

Contents

Propaganda on Film
A Nation at War

PART ONE

The Concept of Propaganda
and the Impact of Film

Characteristics of Propaganda
Jacques Ellul
(1965)

True modern propaganda can only function within the context of the modern scientific system. But what is it? Many observers look upon propaganda as a collection of "gimmicks" and of more or less serious practices. And psychologists and sociologists very often reject the scientific character of these practices. For our part, we completely agree that propaganda is a technique rather than a science. But it is a *modern* technique—that is, it is based on one or more branches of science. Propaganda is the expression of these branches of science; it moves with them, shares in their successes, and bears witness to their failures. The time is past when propaganda was a matter of individual inspiration, personal subtlety, or the use of unsophisticated tricks. Now science has entered propaganda, as we shall reveal from four different points of view.

First of all, modern propaganda is based on scientific analyses of psychology and sociology. Step by step, the propagandist builds his techniques on the basis of his knowledge of man, his tendencies, his desirés, his needs, his psychic mechanisms, his conditioning—and as much on social psychology as on depth psychology. He shapes his procedures on the basis of our knowledge of groups and their laws of formation and dissolution, of mass influences, and of environmental limitations. Without the scientific research of modern psychology and sociology there would be no propaganda, or rather we still would be in the primitive stages of propaganda that existed in the time of Pericles or Augustus. Of course, propagandists may be insufficiently versed in these branches of science; they may misunderstand them, go beyond the cautious conclusions of the psychologists, or claim to apply certain psychological discoveries that, in fact, do not apply at all. But all this only shows efforts to find new ways: only for the past fifty years have men sought to apply the psychological and sociological sciences. The important thing is that propaganda has decided to submit itself to science and to make use of it. Of course, psychologists may be scandalized and say that this is a misuse of their science. But this argument carries no weight; the same applies to our physicists and the atomic bomb. The scientist should know that he lives in a world in which his discoveries will be utilized. Propagandists inevitably will have a better understanding of sociology and psychology, use them with increasing precision, and as a result become more effective.

Second, propaganda is scientific in that it tends to establish a set of rules, rigorous, precise, and tested, that are not merely recipes but impose themselves on every propagandist, who is less and less free to follow his own impulses. He must apply, increasingly and exactly, certain precise formulas that can be applied by anybody with the proper training—clearly a characteristic of a technique based on science.

Third, what is needed nowadays is an exact analysis of both the environment and the individual to be subjected to propaganda. No longer does the man of talent determine the method, the approach, or the subject; all that is now being calculated (or must be calculated). Therefore, one type of propaganda will be found suitable in one situation and completely useless in another. To undertake an active propaganda operation, it is necessary to make a scientific, sociological, and psychological analysis first, and then utilize those branches of science, which are becoming increasingly well known. But, here again, proper training is necessary for those who want to use them with their full effectiveness.

Finally, one last trait reveals the scientific character of modern propaganda: the increasing attempt to control its use, measure its results, define its effects. This is very difficult, but the propagandist is no longer content to have obtained, or to believe he has obtained, a certain result; he seeks precise evidence. Even successful political results do not completely satisfy him. He wants to understand the how and why of them and measure their exact effect. He is prompted by a certain spirit of experimentation and a desire to ponder the results. From this point on, one can see the beginning of scientific method. Admittedly, it is not yet very widespread, and those who analyze results are not active propagandists but philosophers. Granted, that reveals a certain division of labor, nothing more. It indicates that propaganda is no longer a self-contained action, covering up for evil deeds. It is an object of serious thought, and proceeds along scientific channels.

Some people object to this. One frequently hears psychologists ridicule the claim to a scientific basis advanced by the propagandist and reject the latter's claims of having employed scientific techniques. "The psychology he uses is not scientific psychology; the sociology he uses is not scientific sociology." But after a careful look at the controversy one comes to this conclusion: Stalinist propaganda was in great measure founded on Pavlov's theory of the conditioned reflex. Hitlerian propaganda was in great measure founded on Freud's theory of repression and libido. American propaganda is founded in great measure on Dewey's theory of teaching. Now, if a psychologist does not accept the idea of the conditioned reflex and doubts that it can be created in man, he then rejects Pavlov's interpretation of psychological phenomena and concludes that all propaganda based on it is pseudo-scientific. It is obviously the same for those who question the findings of Freud, Dewey, or anybody else.

What does this mean, then? That propaganda does *not* rest on a scientific base? Certainly not. Rather, that scientists are not agreed among themselves on the domains, methods, or conclusions of psychology and sociology. A psychologist who rejects the theory of one of his colleagues rejects a scientific theory and not merely the inferences that a technician may draw from it. One cannot blame the propagandist if he has confidence in a particular sociologist or psychologist whose theory is generally accepted and who is, at a given time and in a given country, considered a scientist. Moreover, let us not forget that if this theory, put to use by the propagandist, brings results and proves to be effective, it thereby receives additional confirmation and that simple doctrinal criticism can then no longer demonstrate its inaccuracy.

Any modern propaganda will, first of all, address itself at one and the same time to the individual and to the masses. It cannot separate the two elements. For propaganda to address itself to the individual, in his isolation, apart from the crowd, is impossible. The individual is of no interest to the propagandist; as an isolated unit he presents much too much resistance to external action. To be effective, propaganda cannot be concerned with detail, not only because to win men over one by one takes much too long, but also because to create certain convictions in an isolated individual is much too difficult. Propaganda ceases where simple dialogue begins. And that is why, in particular, experiments undertaken in the United States to gauge the effectiveness of certain propaganda methods or arguments on isolated individuals are not conclusive: they do not reproduce the real propaganda situation. Conversely, propaganda does not aim simply at the mass, the crowd. A propaganda that functioned only where individuals are gathered together would be incomplete and insufficient. Also, any propaganda aimed only at groups as such—as if a mass were a specific body having a soul and reactions and feelings entirely different from individuals' souls reactions and feelings—would be an abstract propaganda that likewise would have no effectiveness. Modern propaganda reaches individuals enclosed in the mass and as participants in that mass, yet it also aims at a crowd, but only as a body composed of individuals.

What does this mean? First of all, that the individual never is considered as an individual, but always in terms of what he has in common with others, such as his motivations, his feelings, or his myths. He is reduced to an average; and, except for a small percentage, action based on averages will be effectual. Moreover, the individual is considered part of the mass and included in it (and so far as possible systematically integrated into it), because in that way his psychic defenses are weakened, his reactions are easier to provoke, and the propagandist profits from the process of diffusion of emotions through the mass, and, at the same time, from the pressures felt by an individual when in a group. Emotionalism, impulsiveness, excess, etc.—all these characteristics of the individual caught up in a mass are well known and very helpful to propaganda. Therefore, the individual must never be considered as being alone; the listener to a radio broadcast, though actually alone, is nevertheless part of a large group, and he is aware of it. Radio listeners have been found to exhibit a mass mentality. All are tied together and constitute a sort of society in which all individuals are accomplices and influence each other without knowing it. The same holds true for propaganda that is carried on by door-to-door visits (direct contacts, petitions for signatures); although apparently one deals here with a single individual, one deals in reality with a unit submerged into an invisible crowd composed of all those who have been interviewed, who are being interviewed, and who will be interviewed, because they hold similar ideas and live by the same myths, and especially because they are targets of the same organism. Being the target of a party or an administration is enough to immerse the individual in that sector of the population which the propagandist has in his sights; this simple fact makes the individual part of the mass. He is no longer Mr. X, but part of a current flowing in a particular direction. The current flows through the canvasser (who is not a person speaking in his own name with his own arguments, but one segment of an administration, an organization, a collective movement); when he enters a room to canvass a person, the mass, and moreover the organized, leveled mass, enters with him. No relationship exists here between man and man; the organization is what exerts its attraction on an individual already part of a mass because he is in the same sights as all the others being canvassed.

Conversely, when propaganda is addressed to a crowd, it must touch each individual in that crowd, in that whole group. To be effective, it must give the impression of being personal, for we must never forget that the mass is composed of individuals, and is in fact nothing but assembled individuals. Actually, just because men are in a group, and therefore weakened, receptive, and in a state of psychological regression, they pretend all the more to be "strong individuals." The mass man is clearly subhuman, but pretends to be superman. He is more suggestible, but insists he is more forceful; he is more unstable, but thinks he is firm in his convictions. If one openly treats the mass as a mass, the individuals who form it will feel themselves belittled and will refuse to participate. If one treats these individuals as children (and they are children because they are in a group), they will not accept their leader's projections or identify with him. They will withdraw and we will not be able to get anything out of them. On the contrary, each one must feel individualized, each must have the impression that *he* is being looked at, that *he* is being addressed personally. Only then will he respond and cease to be anonymous (although in reality remaining anonymous).

Thus all modern propaganda profits from the structure of the mass, but exploits the individual's need for self-affirmation; and the two actions must be conducted jointly, simultaneously. Of course this operation is greatly facilitated by the existence of the modern mass media of communication, which have precisely this remarkable effect of reaching the whole crowd all at once, and yet reaching each one in that crowd. Readers of the evening paper, radio listeners, movie or TV viewers certainly constitute a mass that has an organic existence, although it is diffused and not assembled at one point. These individuals are moved by the same motives, receive the same impulses and impressions, find themselves focused on the same centers of interest, experience the same feelings, have generally the same order of reactions and ideas, participate in the same myths—and all this at the same time: what we have here is really a psychological, if not a biological mass. And the individuals in it are modified by this existence, even if they do not know it. Yet each one is alone—the newspaper reader, the radio listener. He therefore feels himself individually concerned as a person, as a participant. The movie spectator also is alone; though elbow to elbow with his neighbors, he still is, because of the darkness and the hypnotic attraction of the screen, perfectly alone. This is the situation of the "lonely crowd," or of isolation in the mass, which is a natural product of present-day society and which is both used and deepened by the mass media. The most favorable moment to seize a man and influence him is when he is alone in the mass: it is at this point that propaganda can be most effective.

We must emphasize this circle which we shall meet again and again: the structure of present-day society places the individual where he is most easily reached by propaganda. The media of mass communication, which are part of the technical evolution of this society, deepen this situation while making it possible to reach the individual man, integrated in the mass; and what these media do is exactly what propaganda must do in order to attain its objectives. In reality propaganda cannot exist without using these mass media. If, by chance, propaganda is addressed to an organized group, it can have practically no effect on individuals before that group has been fragmented. Such fragmentation can be achieved through action, but it is equally possible to fragment a group by psychological means. The transformation of very small groups by purely psychological means is one of the most important techniques of propaganda. Only when very small groups are thus annihilated, when the individual finds no more defenses, no equilibrium, no resistance exercised by the group to which he belongs, does total action by propaganda become possible.

Propaganda must be total. The propagandist must utilize all of the technical means at his disposal—the press, radio, TV, movies, posters, meetings, door-to-door canvassing. Modern propaganda must utilize *all* of these media. There is no propaganda as long as one makes use, in sporadic fashion and at random, of a newspaper article here, a poster or a radio program there, organizes a few meetings and lectures, writes a few slogans on walls; that is not propaganda. Each usable medium has its own particular way of penetration—specific, but at the same time localized and limited; by itself it cannot attack the individual, break down his resistance, make his decisions for him. A movie does not play on the same motives, does not produce the same feelings, does not provoke the same reactions as a newspaper. The very fact that the effectiveness of each medium is limited to one particular area clearly shows the necessity of complementing it with other media. A word spoken on the radio is not the same, does not produce the same effect, does not have the same impact as the identical word spoken in private conversation or in a public speech before a large crowd. To draw the individual into the net of propaganda, each technique must be utilized in its own specific way, directed toward producing the effect it can best produce, and fused with all the other media, each of them reaching the individual in a specific fashion and making him react anew to the same theme—in the same direction, but *differently.*

Thus one leaves no part of the intellectual or emotional life alone; man is surrounded on all sides—man and men, for we must also bear in mind that these media do not all reach the same public in the same way. Those who go to the movies three times a week are not the same people who read the newspapers with care. The tools of propaganda are thus oriented in terms of their public and must be used in a concerted fashion to reach the greatest possible number of individuals. For example, the poster is a popular medium for reaching those without automobiles. Radio newscasts are listened to in the better circles. . . .

Each medium is particularly suited to a certain type of propaganda. The movies and human contacts are the best media for sociological propaganda in terms of social climate, slow infiltration, progressive inroads, and over-all integration. Public meetings and posters are more suitable tools for providing shock propaganda, intense but temporary, leading to immediate action. The press tends more to shape general views; radio is likely to be an instrument of international action and psychological warfare, whereas the press is used domestically. In any case, it is understood that because of this specialization not one of these instruments may be left out: they must *all* be used in combination. The propagandist uses a keyboard and composes a symphony.

It is a matter of reaching and encircling the whole man and all men. Propaganda tries to surround man by all possible routes, in the realm of feelings as well as ideas, by playing on his will or on his needs, through his conscious and his unconscious, assailing him in both his private and his public life. It furnishes him with a complete system for explaining the world, and provides immediate incentives to action. We are here in the presence of an organized myth that tries to take hold of the entire person. Through the myth it creates, propaganda imposes a complete range of intuitive knowledge, susceptible of only one interpretation, unique and one-sided, and precluding any divergence. This myth becomes so powerful that it invades every area of consciousness, leaving no faculty or motivation intact. It stimulates in the individual a feeling of exclusiveness, and produces a biased attitude. The myth has such motive force that, once accepted, it controls the whole of the individual, who becomes immune to any other influence. This explains the totalitarian attitude that the individual adopts—wherever a myth has been successfully created—and that simply reflects the totalitarian action of propaganda on him. . . .

Sorcerers or Apprentices:
Some Aspects of the Propaganda Film

Robert Vas

(1963)

Propaganda, we tend to think, is something we live with, inevitable and inescapable. The Central European proverb "I caught a Turk—he won't let me go" fits the situation perfectly. The word "propaganda" has acquired all sorts of overtones during the last quarter of a century; and along with this extension of meaning has grown up that basic mistrust which is our only weapon of defense against it. What on earth could be more suspect than film propaganda? Cinema itself may be called a cheat against reality, but the way the propaganda film operates is a double cheat—it is, in effect, nothing but the sad story of how they've pulled the wool over our eyes.

To raise the moral issues and contradictions involved in this kind of film is yet another task. Did it fertilize the art of the cinema, or work against it? Did it liberate or shackle cinema's powers of expression? We are bound to ask more questions than we can hope to answer. But this article is intended as a sort of subjective reconnaissance of only a few aspects of the subject, mainly those concerned with the creative side rather than with the equally important questions of audience response. Enough if it helps to prepare the ground for a more disciplined and organized attack on this contradictory and menacing subject.

[John] Grierson's[1] classic definition, "Propaganda is the art of public persuasion," does justice to the concept and views it with patience and hope. But this was written in the early thirties, when propaganda films in Britain meant socially conscious educational material about aero-engines, slums, or the six-thirty postal collection. To propagate was the same as to sow the seed of general knowledge. With the film "a single say-so can be repeated a thousand times a night to a million eyes. It opens a new perspective, a new hope to public persuasion." One cannot but feel a certain nostalgia for this period when all our handy definitions were born; when such concepts were still pure and uncorrupted, offering themselves up to clear-cut classification.

As early as 1931, Paul Rotha had enough apt examples to lay down a categorization which is still perfectly valid. "Film propaganda," he wrote in *Celluloid, The Film Today*, "may be said to fall roughly under two heads. Firstly, there is the film which wields influence by reason of its incidental *background* propaganda. Secondly, there is the *specifically designed* propaganda film, sponsored as an advertisement for some industry or policy." And it was in the same essay that he put into words the idea that inevitably comes to mind

---

1. Noted expert on the documentary film.

Reprinted from *Sight and Sound* (1963), pp. 199-204, with permission of the author and the publisher.

when thinking about this subject: "In one form or another, directly or in-directly, *all films are propagandist*. The general public is influenced by every film it sees. The dual physio-psychological appeal of pictorial movement and sound is so strong that if it is made with imagination and skill, the film can stir the emotions of any audience." John Grierson put it all more dramatically: "No form of description," he wrote, "can add nobility to a simple observation so readily as a camera set low or a sequence cut to a time-beat."

This is why film and propaganda *had* to meet. Cinema is reality sifted, pointed and intensified; propaganda is a sifted, pointed, intensified idea used for a specific purpose. And their cooperation was a genuinely mutual one. First involuntarily, then more and more consciously, they have always leaned on each other. When cinema first became aware of its own language and power, it was, in fact, through propaganda. From then on its great moments were also those of the "art of persuasion."

Perhaps it all began with the committed way [*The*] *Birth of a Nation* was put together: the construction of, say, the scene of Lincoln's murder, provoking hatred for the assassin and sympathy for the unsuspecting President. The scene of the liberating Klansmen intercut with the lynch gang makes an even more outspoken (and in fact contradictory) propagandist statement. . . . It was the young Soviet cinema which used it first, along with all those other methods which the textbooks call the basic principles of the art of the film. In Eisen-stein's *Strike*[2] (1924) we find the first intuitive, crude formulation of almost everything that has followed up to the present day, from the sheer elementary power of moving images to the most complex metaphors and abstractions.

It was an intellectual urge which made Eisenstein seek out this language; but he was also a propagandist in those days, even a pamphleteer. It was the effort to achieve propagandist simplicity that encouraged him to think in symbols like The Capitalist and The Proletarian—and so to explore for the first time the cinema's ability (and in a way necessity) to work in terms of types. It was the loose, undisciplined . . . propaganda which enabled him to conceive his film with only an intellectual continuity, and allowed him to ramble freely between the naturalism of the rubber hose sequence and the grotesque and puzzling abstraction of the gnomes, or to link the shot of the slaughtered bull to a clumsily infernal tableau of massacred workers. *Strike* was the first resounding exclamation mark in the history of the cinema, as well as the first haphazard specimen of its intellectual capacities.

Editing, as Eisenstein used it, is a way of showing one's true colors. A cut is a kind of helpful conflict, a harmonic contrast between two shots. A cut in *Potemkin* between the boots of the Czarist troops and the desperately fleeing crowd is a plea in itself: a division between good and evil done with the intensity which only a propaganda film can afford and only a sharp cut can put over. And

---

2. See introduction to Part Two.

From the motion picture **Potemkin.** Courtesy of Museum of Modern Art.

it was out of this propagandist immediacy that one of the cinema's most versatile and dynamic means of expression emerged.

This was the first common ground between film and propaganda, and led to the first turning-point in their history. Before *Potemkin,* film propaganda was used only rather intuitively. Through the artistic success of Eisenstein's film the Soviet cinema became aware of its own possibilities as a worldwide propagandist, and from then on developed them consciously. Even the Master himself could afford to ramble freely within the enormous and more propaganda-conscious concept of his masterpiece, *October,*[3] only after *Potemkin* had shown what could be achieved. . . .

3. Also entitled *Ten Days That Shook the World.*

The West, too, found similar common grounds. *All Quiet on the Western Front* in a way summed up the American cinema and foreshadowed the increasing social awareness of the thirties. In Britain, the propagandist impulse gave the Griersonians their "generous access to the public." Buñuel made propaganda when he explored the horrors of *Las Hurdes*. And in the Germany of the Weimar Republic propaganda was the essence and spice of artistic expression, through the idealistic plea for poor *Mutter Krausen*, through a Brechtian stylization of Rich and Poor, through the sober realism of *Westfront 1918* and the conscious message of *Kameradschaft*. In Mother Russia the Dovzhenko of *Earth* and *Ivan* used propaganda to achieve ends more personal than those desired by the regime, but there is otherwise much to criticize or disregard in Soviet cinema, until *Chapayev* found a way to combine the useful with the truthful. In these years it really does seem true that "all films are propagandist," whether knowingly or unknowingly. The hit song in *42nd Street*, "I'm Young and Healthy, Full of Vitamin A," was like a sad dedication for a world running full speed towards a new war; and the puckish ingenuity of Disney's *Three Little Pigs* helped America to confront the Big Bad Wolf of the Depression. The artistic conscience still dared to hope that it could help.

Then comes the paradox, so sad and so revealing. Though propaganda in the early thirties was conscientiously aimed at social progress, the period's crowning achievement is at once a powerful rebuff and a Machiavellian masterpiece. With *Triumph of the Will* (1934-36) education turned to deliberate misteaching, and the whole idea of propaganda moved towards the era of Goebbels and notoriety.

Leni Riefenstahl's film was a diabolic combination of reality and stylization, Wagnerian mysticism and present-day immediacy, beauty and threat, commanding *tableaux vivants* and an overpowering urgency of movement. Above all, it was a masterpiece of timing. What makes a propagandist film truly great is perhaps this recognition of the right moment, the precise point at which it can assert itself most forcefully. Miss Riefenstahl aimed the superman idea towards that man-in-the-street who, in a confused and disillusioned Europe, was almost waiting for an order to obey. Propaganda had meant goodwill, generalized humanism with all its limitations. Against this, Leni Riefenstahl's film set a firm statement, replacing doubt by military certainty, problems and hesitations by an unambiguous exclamation mark. People who saw the film must have felt that when those in charge were so *sure* about where to put the camera, they could not but be right. . . .

But *Triumph of the Will* also came as a reminder that the real propaganda film can't stand half-measures. It cannot really afford to let us think, and is consequently a totalitarian form of expression. After the final fadeout we are supposed to go straight into action, to seize the nearest spade and begin to dig. . . . Propaganda may have helped Eisenstein to contribute in a general sense to the language of the cinema, but in *Triumph of the Will* Miss Riefenstahl went right back to the core: she liberated the elemental power of direct propaganda and crystallized its full meaning. Her film makes everything that had gone before look merely committed or argumentative. While making full use of Eisenstein's techniques for pictorial rhythm, his flair for symbols or the handling of crowds, she cheerfully rejects his intellectual conscience. To hell with it! Let's have the *real* stuff! And instead of the Master's sophisticated exclamation marks (put down, one feels, with a gold-nibbed fountain-pen on fine paper), here boots thunder out the message on the Nuremberg pavement. (This image of marching boots, indeed, could be taken as the trade mark of the propaganda film: it keeps popping up regularly every ten years.) Here was sheer pagan pomp, shorn of the ballast of humanitarian mental reservations. Reality and symbol walk in step with each other to a thunderous marching rhythm, and for the first time history is used in a direct way to shape history.

Editing, too, takes on a different role. Soldiers marching down a street may be just a bunch of men, but a film shot of their trampling boots expresses *power.* So the editor doesn't give a damn about hidden visual connections, about contrasts or intellectual metaphors. His job is to perform a "simple" cheat: to make two boots out of one, and a victorious regiment with an ideology out of a few lines of marching soldiers. And indeed if those boots, so irresistibly aligned by the editor's scissors, had marched down from the screen, Europe would have been trampled under within a week. . . .

This, then, was the ultimate: something that holds together what has been achieved before, and finds its consummation in a dazzling display which can lead nowhere (except to imitation). *The Triumph of the Will* was really the Defeat of our Infallibility: a symbol of how propaganda has contributed to the natural language of the cinema and led it, simultaneously, to the brink of an abyss of difficult moral questions.

The film made us aware, as nothing else could have done, that here we have a dangerous weapon which can easily misfire. The genie had at last escaped from the tiny bottle and loomed over our heads, monstrous and powerful, ready to carry out any service—if we knew how to handle it. Intellectual and artistic conscience was bound to ask itself whether we are masters of our own strength, or merely the sorcerer's troubled apprentices.

One question mark begets another. Isn't it opposed to the essence of art, which searches for a *universal* truth, to lift out one single, allegedly useful truth and use it perhaps to subvert others? Is such a violent and arbitrary shaping of reality simply immoral, a misuse of democratic ideals? Or can it, because of its crisp immediacy, help to fertilize a vigorous, committed form of artistic expression? Is it a good or an unhealthy sign, for instance, that the same single image of the Nuremberg Rally can be used by Miss Riefenstahl for agitation, then in the British *Swinging the Lambeth Walk* as a piece of scathing irony; that many years later it can be applied (by the Thorndikes, in East Germany) as Communist propaganda, and that finally (after 27 years!) it can be used by Erwin Leiser in an attempt at sober evaluation?

If I feel that everyone must find his own answers to such questions, this is not an evasion. The answers depend largely on personal judgments about aesthetics and politics, on whether one sees art as firmly rooted in its own age or floating in the vacuum of the absolute. The artist, we said, searches for "a universal truth"—but is there any such thing? Everything that rises to the level of artistic truth is bound also to be a private truth, something which the artist has first recognized for himself and to which he gives a new and personal meaning. And who can tell, in any case, where art ends and propaganda begins? After the war neo-realism turned a clean page, trying to rehabilitate this whole besmirched concept, to look for the universal truths and to assert its genuine commitments. But again comes the question: where is the borderline between a propagandist and a committed cinema, and does it even exist? Whenever a cinema becomes socially conscious, sooner or later it is bound to be transformed into propaganda.... Commitment seems to be the word which legitimizes propaganda. But art is an outcome of an immense will to communication. And involvement—why whitewash it?—*is* propaganda.

There may be a difference, though. One may well expect honesty from a committed artist, but not necessarily from the maker of a direct propaganda film. The product is of too dubious a moral value. Yet the question remains worth asking: is it necessary for the propagandist-artist to believe in what he or she is doing? Miss Riefenstahl has repeatedly declared that she knew nothing about the objects of the Nuremberg Rally film—and yet she was able to blend the work of 120 people over a two-year creative period into a breathtaking artistic unity. Can we believe her? Can the thing be done by sheer talent alone? And do we have here a case of intensified commitment or just another monumental and painfully absurd cheat? The moral wilderness of film propaganda is certainly the worst place in which to look for artistic absolutes. Its language has been polished through upholding the bloodiest ideas of mankind, and it seems a fitting product of a world in which it takes an almost physical effort to remain neutral.

Let us grant, however, that it may be possible. And even if all art is more or less propaganda, we can still ask in reverse whether propaganda is art. Many people would give a negative answer. If we *do* live in such circumstances, they would argue, amidst such unstable social, moral, and aesthetic values, then that is all the more reason for the artist to remain impartial. But for the artist to seal himself hermetically into a baroque castle and float in a dream world of the absolute seems to me a blind, cowardly and comfortable form of self-deception. And it strikes me as a kind of propaganda in itself—perhaps the worst kind. It talks about an attitude which it lacks the guts to uphold. The involved artist is concerned to strip life bare and to take his chances; but the other will prefer to dress up a skeleton in decorative clothing. He may find many "absolute" qualities in the *mise en scène* of *Triumph of the Will:* for him art creates its own laws and these justify its aims. But this, it seems to me, is the attitude of the intellectual *Übermensch.*[4] And there isn't a baroque castle on earth, or any laws of art, which could hold out against those marching boots.

---

4. Superman.

There is a fascinating dialectic to be observed in the question of how far propaganda is a product of its times and how far it can influence them. Political and social circumstances may produce an artist who exerts an influence (as Miss Riefenstahl's film doubtless did); the circumstances then change, and the new situation throws up its counter-artists. The very intensity of the propaganda genre means that it carries its own antidotes with it, so that each period seems to fight out its own particular battle between two different kinds of propaganda. Early Nazi films find their opposition (only seemingly indirect) in *L'Espoir* or *La Grande Illusion*. In the moral wilderness there is still a continuous line pursued by the progressive conscience: in post-war documentaries about hunger and want; in neo-realist films standing for basic human rights; in the conscience of American journalistic films during the McCarthyist era; in the intellectualism of the French documentarists; in the attack against old standards by the Free Cinema group. Such continuous conflict is one of the things that helps to keep the genre alive.

It is typical of the anarchistic rootlessness of film propaganda (and a compliment, too, to its versatility) that its greatest works have a way of emerging from what seem to be the least promising circumstances. Eisenstein's intellectualism came out of (and almost in spite of) a bloody revolution. Riefenstahl's work emerged from (and against) the desperately humanist atmosphere of the thirties. And out of the Second World War came the incarnation of the humanist artist, a poet as noble, mature, and controlled as Humphrey Jennings.[5]

Jennings' subjective style was perfected at precisely the moment when the general language of the propaganda film was at its most direct. War seems to be the test, to some extent even the harvest, of propaganda. Both involve uncompromising and totalitarian concepts. And to loosen up such a state of emergency in the arts, at a time when everything is gauged to the tight bark of a military command, is in itself an act of real courage. But this kind of liberation, with its rejection of all imperative symbols, was precisely the essence of Jennings' art. He recognized that true patriotism (and also good propaganda) can have its roots in the conscious temper of the people rather than the showy trappings. Riefenstahl tramples her awed audience underfoot; Jennings lifts them up again into humanity. Riefenstahl's propaganda quickly exhausts the few superficial symbols of its ideology; Jennings looks for the inner heartbeat of his country in troop trains, factory canteens, wheatfields, fire stations, National Gallery concerts. At long last propaganda was flowing again from the most intimate beliefs and visions of an artist. Even the most stubborn purists might be reassured that public persuasion *can* be an art.

For the umpteenth time in its own history alone, *montage* once more takes on a different role. For the old trickery of two-boots-for-the-price-of-one, Jennings substitutes something much more flexible. Like a Debussy or a Renoir,

---

5. Director of several British war propaganda films.

he finds fresh associations of pictures and sounds, discovers an airy music of images to mirror a sea of moods, connections, contrasts, episodes in the life of his country at war. The historic moment creates its own symbols: a barrage balloon; Myra Hess playing Beethoven ("German music"); the bare, empty walls of the National Gallery. For the poet, these are simply observations made in a particular context: nothing and therefore everything. And perhaps this is why, once the war was over and the intensity of the circumstances had vanished, Jennings could never really recapture this rare poetic amalgam of the ordinary and the extraordinary.

Similar contradictions are apparent in the screen propaganda of the present day. As the world political climate became more and more gloomy during the fifties, so film propaganda grew scared of its own power and responsibility. Soft, mild, middle-of-the-road film-making became the style. The political situation, fertilizer of propagandist art, was itself too desperate, and faced with the elemental problem of sheer survival everything became ridiculously over-simplified. Symbols seem to be produced on the assembly line, and concepts like The Bomb, The Wall, The Button themselves neutralize any kind of artificial symbolism which propaganda could provide. The marching boots of the old stereotype simply can't keep up any longer. Nor, I think, would Jennings' gentle poetry be able to catch up with and confront the situation. And while on the surface things may appear to be over-simplified, beneath this surface the atmosphere is more confused and complex than ever.

The easy way is to make the most of the simplified situation by accepting it at face value. It has become too easy for anyone with a few sympathetically progressive ideas to become a passionate benefactor of mankind. . . . Make a neutral film about the last people surviving on earth, première it in a 15-nation saturation booking, and you become the greatest prophet that money can buy. Make a film about Innocent Blond Ivan caught up in the Inhumanities of War, and you will win all the top prizes at San Francisco. . . .

But perhaps we help to foster this image by ourselves becoming gradually more and more immune to human misery. In Japan they have made a wide-screen, color, stereophonic epic about the annihilation of mankind by nuclear war, addressed (as a new type of publicity stunt) directly to Messrs. Khrushchev and Kennedy. Even in the thirties this could have seemed a disturbing, thought-provoking Wellsian vision: now we just smile at it and make a quick comment on the clumsiness of the special effects . . . And why not? We can watch the genuine real-life horror, all the painful superlatives which our contemporary existence can produce, at home in our slippers, after tea. And after close-ups of the killing at Leopoldville; the earthquake in Iran; the public execution of a head of state in a television studio, all laid at our feet by the unsurpassable magic of the telephoto lens and the cathode ray tube, what price a *Las Hurdes* in the cinema?

Yet here seems to be the root, and also the solution of the problem. Great things may have become everyday things; the capital letters may have been hacked to death. Isn't this, then, the precise moment when an artist should step in, should reassess the bloated and overworked concepts by subjecting them to his own personal viewpoint, treating them with that indefinable plus quality that only an artist can contribute? It is impossible to intensify the exclamation mark slammed down by a single shot of a heap of human hair at Auschwitz—but at the same time it *can* be intensified into a *Night and Fog*. . . .

True, it is a question whether this long overdue invasion of conscience, and the return to an Eisensteinian intellectual humanism, may bring death or regeneration to this fundamentally totalitarian form of expression. A few years ago many devotees of the genre praised to the skies the effective Communist propaganda films made in East Germany by the Thorndikes. Perhaps they seemed like the last of the Mohicans: the defenders of the "real stuff." But, I feel, the quieter, sometimes hesitant, voice of awakening conscience means much more now than a few smart pranks with the editor's scissors or some bombastically effective pictorial harangue.

Perhaps the whole concept of film propaganda, in itself and in relation to its audience, will soon have to be reassessed. Films by Chris Marker and Jean Rouch[6] illustrate the close links with television, but also the film's own superiority to it. In these works, at long last, propaganda is being written in lower case rather than in the old capital letters. And at a time when history so visibly outruns us, is formed, reformed and indeed deformed before our eyes, the real aim of propaganda ought to be to determine (and no longer to confuse) the place and role of human beings in our topsy-turvy universe. It's in this way that the genre could be rehabilitated.

But in the meantime there is something we can benefit from right now. If propaganda, with all its dangers, reminds us of the need to face up to the world we live in, urges us not to remain neutral but to try to adopt a standpoint, then let it come. It will help us to build up our own resistance. After all, it was *we* who allowed ourselves to be cheated.

---

6. French documentary film-makers.

FOR DISCUSSION

1. After reading the "characteristics" of all propaganda by Jacques Ellul, consider the extent to which these apply to cinematic propaganda. Has film propaganda been scientifically applied? Has the film propaganda of some societies (Soviet Russia or Nazi Germany, for example) been applied more scientifically than their American counterpart? Consider these factors as you read through the rest of this text.

2. Film historian Robert Vas notes that even though there is a separate category of motion pictures which is specifically designed for propaganda, technically, "all films are propagandist." Consider the implications of this further. Think of the last film you went to see for "pure" entertainment. How could it be interpreted as propaganda? What point of view was it "selling"? Did it flaunt any particular life style? Did it contain any definable attitudes toward any of our basic institutions—male-female relationships, economic affluence, or generational differences? If it was a comedy, what was the source of its humor? (At whose expense were many of the jokes made?) What kind of attitudes are being sold with a film like *Love Story,* for example? As you get deeper into this text, note how specific political and social ideas could be integrated into standard, entertainment movies for propaganda purposes.

3. Toward the conclusion of his article, Robert Vas comments on what he considers the "real aim of propaganda" for our times. At best, his statement is pretty vague. After reading the entire unit, return to Vas's statement to see if it makes more sense. If it does not, state your own "real aim" for propaganda in our society.

PART TWO

The Refinement of
the Art of Cinematic Propaganda—
Early Soviet Russia and Nazi Germany

In the days immediately following the Bolshevik Revolution, the new Soviet government under Vladimir Illyich Lenin sought to harness all of the nation's mass media to propagandize Marxist ideology. The official newspaper, *Pravda,* printed the following statement to that effect in early 1919:

> Political propaganda in the country must be conducted for both the literates and the illiterates. . . . The cinema theatre, concerts, exhibitions, etc., as much as they will penetrate to the country, and towards this end all forces must be applied, must be used for communist propaganda directly. . . .[1]

Lenin was particularly interested in the potential of motion pictures as the most important propaganda medium.[2] Under his leadership, a deeply committed (to Bolshevism) film industry was created to produce films which were both aesthetic masterpieces and great works of propaganda. In the first half of this section, Timothy Angus Jones and Robert Warshow offer contrasting views of the early Soviet cinema from the vantage point of the 1950s.

The second half of Part Two concentrates on the cinematic propaganda of Nazi Germany (which, as you shall see, was heavily influenced by the Soviet model). The films of the German Third Reich (particularly *Triumph of the Will,* analyzed in detail in this section) represent perhaps the most thorough effort of a society to use the cinema for propaganda purposes.

---

1. Quoted from Jay Leyda, *Kino: A History of the Russian and Soviet Film* (N.Y.: The Macmillan Company, 1960), p. 139.
2. In 1919, Lenin saw D. W. Griffith's masterful American film, *Intolerance,* and was so impressed by the power that he offered Griffith full charge of the Russian film industry. Griffith, of course, refused. But from this point on, Lenin sought out the expertise of Soviet film-makers to "sell" Marxism-Leninism to the Russian people. *Ibid.,* pp. 142-143.

"Potemkin" As an Epic

Timothy Angus Jones

(1955)

A Soviet film about a mutiny on a Czarist warship is almost certain to have a political bias, but *The Battleship Potemkin* could never be simply dismissed as propaganda. There is a strong ideological flavour, and it is plain (even without knowing the true history of the mutiny) that the film has "adapted" the truth. But the adaptation seems innocent of a desire to indoctrinate. There are flaws in its story—obvious contradictions, a lame ending, a feeling that the tale is only half-told—that a competent propagandist would surely have avoided. And in spite of these faults, and in spite of the film's immature technique, there is an elevation of spirit that rises above the want of drama and transcends the political bias.

It is almost an "epic" spirit, and the film is not unlike a primitive epic poem; in Homer's *Iliad*, for instance, there is this same combination of majesty, crudeness of treatment, and ideology. The key to the similarity seems to lie in this sense of incompleteness, this feeling that the story is only half-told. For it is as if the tale the film tells is one with which the audience is expected to be already familiar; as if, over the twenty years before the film was made, the story of the *Potemkin* had already become a popular legend.

The film was made in 1925; it is a silent film, without dialogue, but with captions to provide a commentary. The actual mutiny occurred during the Social Democratic revolutionary movement of 1905–1907. It was an isolated incident, however, relatively non-political in origin, and not directly connected with the movement.

The *Prince Potemkin Tauritchesky* was the largest capital ship of the Black Sea Fleet. The mutiny broke out while she was at sea on manoeuvres, escorted by the torpedo boat No. 267. It arose from some putrefying meat, used to make soup for the sailors' midday meal. The complaints of the crew reached the Captain, and they were paraded on the foredeck in the early afternoon. During this parade, aggrieved by their vile conditions of service and provoked by their treatment from their superiors, the crew revolted, seized arms from the guard-room, and murdered the Captain and the senior officers. The torpedo boat followed their example. The ringleaders were two sailors, Vakulintchuk and Matushenko: Vakulintchuk was shot in the first fighting and died the same afternoon; Matushenko set up a committee of the mutineers, and the battleship and her escort turned for Odessa, where (as they had heard) a strike among the factory workers had developed into an insurrection.

From *Encounter,* January 1955, London. Reprinted with permission.

The *Potemkin* dropped anchor off Odessa that evening, and the body of Vakulintchuk was landed in the dark and laid under a tent on the mole, where next morning it attracted an enthusiastic crowd. She anchored there for three days, and received visits from delegates of the local revolutionary organisation. But the mutineers seemed to have no further plans beyond recoaling and taking in a supply of fresh provisions; they were reluctant to leave their fortress to join forces with the strikers on shore; and other than this there was little assistance they could render. In the circumstances the battleship's heavy armament was useless, for they could not bombard the town or engage with the Fleet without killing their own comrades. On the second evening, indeed, two salvoes were fired as a gesture at the military headquarters in Odessa. But except for this, the *Potemkin* remained during her ten days' liberty in a state of helpless rebellion.

On the third day the rest of the squadron arrived from Sevastopol under the command of the Admiral, and the battleship and her torpedo boat stood out to sea. Neither side, however, seemed willing to be the first to open fire, and there followed a bloodless engagement in which the *Potemkin* passed twice through the line of ships without a shot being exchanged. While this was going on there were some demonstrations among the lower decks of the squadron, and the crew of one ship, the *George The Victorious,* put their officers under restraint and went over to the mutineers. The Admiral, fearful of further infection, gave the order to disengage. The *Potemkin* and the *George* returned to port, and the squadron disappeared over the horizon.

The film ends on this indecisive encounter with the squadron. What in fact followed was that next day the *George* regretted her defection, and, after an unsuccessful attempt to escape under the guns of the *Potemkin,* went in alongside the mole. With the harbour occupied by a hostile vessel, Matushenko and the mutineers lost their heads and resolved on flight. The *Potemkin* sailed out of Odessa that evening. For the next few days she cruised up and down the Black Sea, gradually running short of coal; and finally, with her bunkers empty, surrendered on the Rumanian coast. The mutiny was over. Three years later the tide of revolution had receded. Between 1907 and 1917 there was a break in the continuity of the revolutionary movement, and at the time it appeared to be final. One of the delegates from Odessa who visited the battleship, writing an account of the mutiny shortly after, speaks then of the "Russian Revolution" as something which—so far as it went—had already run its course.

The story is not promising material for propaganda: an isolated revolt, ending ingloriously, and wholly unconnected with the victory of the Revolution in 1917. But at the time the mutiny must have stirred the Social Democrats. Stories will have been told about it. Assume that the legend grows. What the bearers of the legend will wish to do is to place the mutiny somewhere in their glorious past; and the legend will try to establish a connection between the mutiny and the Revolution, and to draw the attention away from the larger historical view—and the failure of the mutiny—towards particular aspects of it that caught the imagination at the time.

This is exactly what is done in the film. The elements of the true story are there: the two leaders, Vakulintchuk and Matushenko; the putrid meat; the ship's surgeon staring at the maggots and pronouncing the meat wholesome; the parade and the fighting on the foredeck; Odessa; the curious encounter with the squadron. But the emphasis has been altered; the mutiny becomes part of the Revolution; a spiritual connection is established. It is no longer a spontaneous outbreak. We see the two leaders laying their plans in advance, preparing to act in concert with the strikers of Odessa. Matushenko, who led the revolt after his comrade's death, never appears after the first scene: for it was he who later led the flight to Rumania and betrayed the mutiny. But Vakulintchuk is made a martyr. Long scenes are devoted to the repose of his body on the mole, with the epitaph pinned to his breast—_"For a spoonful of soup"_; the loafers at dawn peering into the tent that covers the bier; the word passed from mouth to mouth, the weeping women, the rising fury; the whole town pouring down to the harbour; and we see in dumb-show the interminable stirring speeches over his corpse that are so familiar from epic poetry. In this way the attention is diverted from the historical setting, and from what happened to the mutiny afterwards. Moreover, the story is left unfinished. The _Potemkin_ steams out to meet the squadron, and there is a silence as she draws near; then a burst of cheering as she begins to pass through the line, and on all the ships the sailors crowd the decks and fling their caps across the water to the glory of the victorious Revolution. And there the film stops. The last picture is of the battleship ploughing irresistibly on towards the audience; and the plain inference is that in a short while she will have ploughed over the last shattered fragments of the Czarist régime. The gap of twelve years to 1917 and the ebbing of the revolutionary tide in the meantime are quietly passed over.

What is striking in the film, however, is that this has not been done more thoroughly. Again and again the revision of history seems to be hampered by an inconvenient scruple for the truth. This occurs in many places where a detail of the true story remains to contradict its "revolutionary" context. It occurs more seriously in the confusion over the immediate cause of the mutiny. Here the film seems to be telling two stories at once. One in which it is a planned movement, initiated by the Social Democrats; and in this story the signal for mutiny is given when Vakulintchuk defiantly leads his comrades off parade, breaking their ranks to take their stand by the gun-turret. And the other in which the mutiny is a spontaneous revolt of the crew over their rations; in this, the true story, the crew break ranks in obedience to an order, and the signal for the fighting comes later; the officers decide to make an example of some of the sailors, and Vaku-lintchuk, in unpremeditated heroism, suddenly steps forward with a cry. The first story clearly suits the revolutionary theme; but no attempt is made to suppress the second, and both versions are given in the film in a disjointed sequence. Again at the end of the film the story is too obviously unfinished. As the _Potemkin_ steams into the squadron every sign prepares us for a spectacular engagement: instead there is a silence, a burst of cheering, and caps thrown into

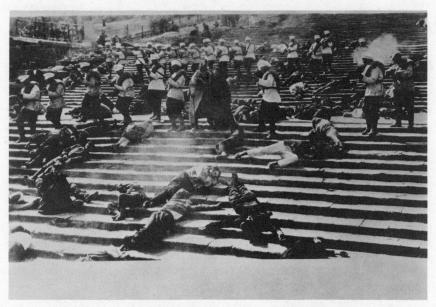

From the motion picture **Potemkin.** Courtesy of Museum of Modern Art.

the sea: nothing more. There is the lamest of attempts to suggest a victory, without actually saying so. And one suspects at once that the inconclusive ending conceals an inglorious sequel.

But this is understandable if the film is the product of a popular legend, a traditional story of the type found in primitive epic poetry. A legend of this type owes its growth and survival to a nostalgia—to a portrayal of a past age or society whose memory is still cherished, or some event of popular significance which for a particular reason is worth recalling. Thus the epic poetry of the Greek and Teutonic peoples each recalled a heroic age, since passed away, separated from the poet by several generations. The legend is an attempt to recapture the lost spirit of the heroic age. In this broad sense its purpose is always ideological: it may intend merely to portray heroic spirit, and not consciously to indoctrinate: but it is not directly concerned with recording history, nor merely with telling a good dramatic story. The story may have no historical significance at all. The siege of Troy left no mark on the political history of Greece; the struggle of an unidentified prehistoric people, the "Achaeans," for the control of a fortress in Asia Minor, a fortress about the size of a medieval castle, and a struggle which probably ended in defeat. But ideologically its influence—through the *Iliad*—was immense. It was the spirit of the *Iliad,* the "Homeric" spirit, which for classical Greece gave significance to the duels of the heroes round the walls of Troy.

But the legend grows slowly, and its growth depends on tradition. At first there may be a number of different versions of the story, conflicting with one another in detail, each incomplete and to some extent still fluid, which will be exposed to the editing of succeeding generations. Then at some stage a definitive version, such as the *Iliad*, comes into being: but by this time the task of its author (or editor) will be a difficult one. So far as he can he will now have to make a good story of it; but he must do justice to the spirit of the legend. Moreover, in each popular version there will be things which have acquired a sanctity of their own: some incident, some vivid detail, that strikes the imagination and suggests the whole story. That was the time (one might remember) when the ship's surgeon refused to see the maggots under his nose. Or that was the time when one of the squadron sailed over to the side of the *Potemkin* . . . . Some of these remembered incidents may be out of place in a dramatic account of the affair. Some may contradict others equally well remembered—was it really the maggots that started the mutiny, or was it the planning of Vakulintchuk? Some of them may have a deeper significance that does violence to the legend—true, the *George The Victorious* sailed over to the mutineers; but in the end her adherence led to disaster, for her treachery next day precipitated the flight that ended in surrender. . . . But each of these memories is fixed in tradition, and all must somehow find their place.

The author of the final version is thus bound by his material. It need not be complete; his audience are already familiar with the story. He may leave out parts of it which do not suit his theme. He may shift the emphasis. But he cannot invent, and he cannot falsify. Where for instance two accounts of a particular incident conflict, neither can be sacrificed; both must be incorporated bodily and somehow harmonised in the text. This happens repeatedly in Homer, in the "spurious" lines and passages which scholars used to reject as contradicting the "genuine" parts of the story. It happens in the film in the two superimposed accounts of the actual mutiny. The method leads to contradictions in the final version, but tradition is satisfied either way: Vakulintchuk is both the scheming revolutionary and also the sudden hero of the moment. And the same kind of method is used in expurgating details which are harmful to the spirit of the legend. There must be the least possible tampering with the story, some incident may have an unpleasant significance, but it is already part of the tradition. And so traces remain—there is a taint on the memory of Matushenko, but tradition remembers him as one of the ringleaders, and he cannot be wholly eliminated. The memory of the *George The Victorious* is also tainted; but the story tells of one of the squadron who went over to the mutineers, and so in the film we find the *George*'s place taken by the torpedo boat No. 267. (This torpedo boat in fact accompanied the battleship from the beginning; but we see her first only at the end of the film, during the encounter with the squadron; and there is an ambiguous caption—"The Destroyer 267, which went over to the insurgents, never left the battleship's side.") And then, to enhance the martyrdom of Vakulintchuk, there is a similar expurgation of the slaughter *en masse* of the ship's officers.

This adaptation of the true story is not a deliberate revision of history. It is a gradual, haphazard process, practically completed before the "final version" comes into being. It is simply that a traditional story, in the retelling, gradually gives more prominence to what best exemplifies its own theme, and innocently omits whatever tradition does not wish to remember. And it is from this process too that the legend ultimately acquires its epic quality. It took several centuries of oral repetition for the *Iliad* to grow out of the tales of the Trojan War, to become the traditional book of the young Greek peoples. With the legend of the *Potemkin* the period is much shorter. In place of a young civilisation there is a political creed still in its infancy: instead of the spirit of a lost heroic age, the young spirit of revolution which in victory has perhaps lost the ardour of its first youth. The spirit is a different one, political rather than ethical; and instead of individual heroes there is the Party and the People. But the stories still have the epic quality; they are still stories of heroes, heroes with whom there is established a definite spiritual ancestry, and whose deeds in the retelling gradually acquire the ideological significance for which the stories have come to be remembered.

If these were the sources of *The Battleship Potemkin*, it can be understood why the film has at first the appearance, but does not leave behind the flavour, of propaganda; for its makers were bound by their material, and the political bias had already been implanted in the material by the processes of tradition. These are the same processes that gave birth to the earliest European poem. And this may explain why, in spite of the flaws in the film's composition and its plainly partisan interpretation of history, it has an unconscious nobility of spirit that is only found in epic literature.

Re-Viewing the Russian Movies

Robert Warshow
(1955)

A curse on all Marxists, and on all those who want to bring into all the relations of life hardness and dryness— Lev Davidovich Bronstein (1896); quoted by Bertram D. Wolfe in *Three Who Made a Revolution*.

Six of the famous movies of the Russian Revolution have been shown recently in New York. Five of them are among the most celebrated products of what we have all agreed to call the great age of the Soviet cinema: Pudovkin's *The End of St. Petersburg,* Dovzhenko's *Earth,* and Eisenstein's *Potemkin, Ten Days That Shook the World,* and *The General Line.* The sixth, *Tsar to Lenin,* is a collection of authentic pictures of actual people and events taken by perhaps a

Reprinted from *The Immediate Experience* by Robert Warshow with permission from Paul Warshow.

hundred different photographers—newsreel and military cameramen and ama-
teurs, including the Czar himself and members of his circle.

I had seen most of these movies at one time or another, but none of them
for at least fifteen years, and I went this time looking very consciously for the
pathos and irony of that enormous historical failure which now weighs so
dangerously on us all. Irony, God knows, was easy enough to find; every glimpse
of the enthusiasms of that revolution brings forth all at once the whole
wearisome joke of human aspiration and wickedness—we shall be having it
dinned into our ears, in just this form, until we die. There was more irony than
the most avid of paradox-mongers could possibly want. Only to see the word
"comrades" or the word "workers" in a subtitle was enough. Before I was
through I could no longer even understand why our age insists on finding the
idea of irony so attractive. I would have given up all ironies, and the sense of
tragedy and the sense of history along with them, just to have stupid, handsome
Nicholas grinding his heel once more into the face of unhappy Russia.

Pathos was another matter. For pathos there must be victims, and in five
of these six movies the glare of triumphant righteousness is so blinding that one
can't see any victims at all, only a few martyrs of the working class, their lives
well expended, and a few bourgeois or monarchist anachronisms, swept properly
into the dustbin of history. No death is without meaning; even that baby
hurtling in its carriage down the Odessa steps in *Potemkin* is part of the great
plan, and the spectacle is exciting but not saddening. Of course it could be said
that Eisenstein and Pudovkin and Dovzhenko were the real victims, ultimately
betrayed by the revolution they celebrated; but that idea, if it is important at all,
becomes important only on reflection. It is hard to feel the pathos of their lives
when you see them playing with corpses; if they had got the chance, they would
have made a handsome montage of my corpse too, and given it a meaning—their
meaning and not mine.

I do not say that these films of the famous Russian directors left me
unmoved, but what I felt was all the wrong things, anger more than anything
else. And it is just the best elements that arouse the greatest anger. When
Eisenstein photographs the slow raising of the bridge in *Ten Days That Shook
the World,* with a dead woman's hair stretched over the crack between the two
sides as they come apart, and a dead horse hanging in its harness higher and
higher above the river as the bridge goes up, the whole slow sequence being
further protracted by the constant cutting in of other shots in "rhythmic"
contrast, these controlled elements that once marked Eisenstein's seriousness as
an artist become now the signs of an essential and dangerous frivolity which, one
suspects, was a part of what made him an artist in the first place (and which is
exhibited also in the intolerable pedantry of his theoretical writings). And when
Pudovkin in *The End of St. Petersburg* cuts rapidly back and forth from scenes
of fighting at the front to scenes of excitement in the stock exchange, one's
anger is mingled with shame: this sequence is mentioned with honor in the
histories of the cinema.

To be honest, I must say that I had come with some hope of finding that the pretensions of the great Soviet cinema were false. Since I had never, in fact, quite accepted those pretensions, it may not count for much to say that these films seemed to me, in aesthetic terms, as successful as ever. But I do mean that they belong with what we are accustomed to call great films, which is to say that they are crude, vulgar, often puerile, but yet full of sudden moments of power. The scene of the Odessa steps, for instance, deserves all the praise that has been given to it, and perhaps even justifies a recent attempt by Timothy Angus Jones (*Encounter,* January 1955) to establish *Potemkin* as an "epic," especially when one recalls that epic is often an expression of barbarism and superstition. It was not at all an aesthetic failure that I encountered in these movies, but something worse: a triumph of art over humanity. It made me, for a while, quite sick of the art of the cinema, and sick also of the people who sat with me in the audience, *mes semblables,* whom I suspected of being either cinema enthusiasts or Communists—and I wasn't always sure which was worse. (In fact the audiences were unusually silent at most of these movies, and for all I know may have been suffering the same emotions as I was.)

It has been said that the great achievement of the early Soviet cinema was its grasp of the impersonal, of the drama of "masses" and "forces." It was a new art, for a new age, in which the individual was seen to have his truest being as part of the mass. The real hero of these movies is history. But if there is one thing we should have learned from history—and from the history of the Russian Revolution above all—it is that history ought to be nobody's hero. When it is made into a hero, it is not even history any more, but falsehood. There is something peculiarly appropriate in Eisenstein's and Pudovkin's fondness for architectural and statuary symbolism. Eisenstein represents the rising of the workers, for instance, with a famous montage of three stone lions, one asleep, the second with its head lifted, and the third rising to its feet; by projecting these images in rapid succession, he creates the impression of a single lion stirred into action. This is another example of montage that is mentioned with honor in the textbooks, usually with the information that the three lions were not even photographed in the same city, a fact which is supposed to cast light on the question of whether the cinema is an art. The use of the stone lion is, indeed, a clever and "artistic" idea, but it is also fundamentally cheap, and in both respects it is characteristic of Eisenstein, and of the Soviet cinema generally. What we want most, that cinema rarely gives us: some hint of the mere reality of the events it deals with. The important point about the lions is that all the "art" of their use depends on the fact that they are not alive.

Against the films of Eisenstein and Pudovkin, *Tsar to Lenin* has at least the advantage of not being a work of art or even, in the usual sense, a documentary. This is not to say that it is completely artless. The material, gathered over a period of years from a multitude of sources, was carefully arranged and, no doubt, carefully selected. The sequences are presented as much as possible in chronological order, and there is a spoken commentary by Max Eastman (the pictures themselves, of course, are without sound). At one point there is even a rudimentary "montage," contrasting the homely and unassuming Kalinin with the aloof and splendidly uniformed Czar. I don't suppose, either, that the process of selection rested solely on the objective interest of the material. It is notable, for instance, that the only pictures of an execution show the shooting of Communist prisoners by soldiers of Kolchak's army; on the Bolshevik side there is only a photograph of the room in which the Czar and his family were killed, and a brief glimpse of the head of the Cheka, identified by the commentator as "the incorruptible Dzerzhinsky." (What can it mean to call a political mass murderer "incorruptible"?) Again, in contrast to *Ten Days That Shook the World*, where the existence of Trotsky is never even acknowledged (except for a brief shot of an unnamed figure with the familiar pointed beard shown vaguely "plotting" against Lenin), this film takes perhaps special care to document as fully as possible Trotsky's role as a Bolshevik leader and as commander of the Red Army; the face of that "bloody-minded professor" is the most persistent image in the film. Nor are we spared the ineffable vulgarities of Communist rhetoric; indeed they are more oppressive here than in the other films because the commentary is spoken and we must endure to hear Max Eastman expressing the sentiments of 1937 in the very tones of 1937. "Kerensky had completely ignored the fundamental demand of the masses." "Lenin explained his purpose to the masses." "Kolchak was totally incapable of understanding the situation." "Trotsky proclaimed: 'Kerensky is a tool of the landlords and capitalists! All power to the Soviet!'" This is the language we once listened to with patience. I would have felt sorry for Max Eastman—who after all made no montages of corpses—if I had not been feeling more sorry for myself. Still, perhaps it would be no better if the sentiments were those of 1955. The commentator is one of the diseases of our time and must be endured; he will be there at the end of the world to say into a microphone: "This is the end of the world." But his greatest power lies not in what he says but in his tone of healthy intelligence; Max Eastman has at any rate a certain nervousness in his speech which makes one wish to forgive him. . . .

1933: The Subversion of the Film Industry

David Stewart Hull
(1969)

[Perhaps the most direct and total use of the film medium as propaganda was by Nazi Germany. The head of its propaganda machine, Joseph Goebbels, heavily influenced by the Russians, was a great believer in the motion picture as a forceful persuader. He took total control of the German film industry (as described by film historian, David Stewart Hull) and used it as a vociferous spokesman for the policies of the Third Reich.

The Nazi propaganda films were of three types: 1. glorification of Adolf Hitler and Nazi principles; 2. anti-Semitism to arouse a "racial-nationalism" among Germans; 3. glorification of German military might. The first two types were geared to domestic audiences while the third was exported to nations ripe for Nazi conquest.]

Film would hardly have played an important part in the history of the Third Reich if it had not been for the presence of Joseph Goebbels in the Party hierarchy. Hitler found films only a pleasant way to relax at the end of the day, and enjoyed the company of pretty actresses in public and private; Göring dabbled in opera and theatre and only took an interest in film when his favorites were involved (his second wife, Emmy Sonnemann, had appeared in a few movies); the remainder of the Party leadership will rarely appear in this history.

Goebbels was not only interested in but almost obsessed by films. There probably has never been another individual in the history of any modern government who devoted so much of his time to the motion picture in every possible capacity. It is startling to realize that every film made in the Third Reich had to be passed by Goebbels for public showing, including features, shorts, newsreels, and documentaries.

The reasons for Goebbels' enthusiasm for the film medium are not too hard to find. Of course, he realized the value of film as propaganda for the Nazi party, but the reasons go deeper. As a young man he was a writer and was fascinated by the stage and its actors. He grew up during the period when German films gradually gained supremacy in Europe, and their influence was felt throughout the world. Unlike most Nazi leaders, he was a well-educated and well-read man. And he was, to some extent, stagestruck.

However, nature had seen to it that he would not be an actor. An early illness had left him with a deformed foot, and he walked with a limp which he managed to minimize with great difficulty. He was short, and not particularly good looking. With these physical limitations, he attempted to enter the cultural

Originally published by the University of California Press; reprinted by permission of The Regents of the University of California.

world as an author, but his early works were turned down. The frustrations of an ambitious young man in these situations can be well imagined.

To compensate for some of these physical factors he worked on his voice. There was an initial problem here because he was a Rhinelander, with an accent which tends to be somewhat amusing to the average German. With much hard work he eliminated this and gradually developed one of the most remarkable voices in the history of modern politics.

It was a voice which cannot be described in words. Recordings do it some justice, but only in films, coupled with his demonic personal presence, can it be fully appreciated. It is not necessary to understand German to get the message of his speeches; the inflection, the modulation in a single syllable could turn a passive audience into a screaming mob. Through hard practice he was able to perfect a delivery which was equally impressive to huge gatherings and to the radio audience at home. As a public speaker, Goebbels had no peer.

Yet despite this remarkable gift, there was still a gnawing sense of inferiority underneath his snappy, fast-talking façade. He went out of his way to cultivate friends in the theatre and film circles, and not only because they could be of help to him in his political projects. His attitude toward these persons bordered on worship. They could in theory do no wrong. Many an erring actor or actress found a personal scandal hushed up by the personal intervention of Goebbels in his years of power. As his aid Rudolf Semmler observed. "His motto is like that of Frederick the Great: 'Artists must not be bothered.' "

The career of Goebbels has been well documented in a number of books, and his rapid rise in the political world of national socialism can be found elsewhere. Throughout his life, Goebbels kept detailed diaries, although the bulk of them vanished, apparently to points East, in the final days of Berlin. These diaries were meant for future publication, and parts of them have already reached us in various states. The first diary that concerns us covers the period of 1932–1933 and was prepared for publication by Goebbels under the title *Vom Kaiserhof zur Reichskanzlei* (1934). The period of 1942–1943 is covered in a book edited by Louis Lochner under the title *The Goebbels Diaries* (1948).

What is striking about these books is the amount of material relating to films. Even on the busiest day, Goebbels found time to see at least one film, and apparently to write about it. There are facts about the films of the time, gossip about this or that actress, and occasional flights of fancy on the future of the medium. Goebbels' interest in the motion picture went far beyond that of a "hobby" as some commentators have referred to it. He probably understood films as well as any industry executive, and probably better. . . .

Triumph of the Will —
An Outline

[In 1934, a young actress-film-maker named Leni Riefenstahl was commissioned by Adolf Hitler to make an elaborate documentary film of the proposed Nazi Party Rally at Nuremberg. The rally was to be a pageant celebrating the vast power of National Socialism (and to demonstrate party unity after the purging of Ernst Rohm and his storm troop faction). The entire city of Nuremberg was put at her disposal, and virtually all of the pageantry of the rally itself (triumphant parades of uniformed "Aryans" and swastika banners, torch lighting ceremonies, etc.) was consciously staged to be filmed. Miss Riefenstahl had all of the technology of the German cinema at her disposal, and the film certainly shows it. Historian David Stewart Hull's evaluation of *Triumph of the Will* truly sums up its power as propaganda:

"The purpose of the film was twofold: to show Germans the solidarity of the Party, particularly following the divisions caused by the Rohm affair; and to introduce the leaders, many of whom spoke a few words, to this pre-television society. Another, more subtle purpose was to impress foreign audiences, and at the same time to scare the hell out of them. The film succeeded on all counts."[1]

Reprinted here is a scenario-outline of *Triumph of the Will,* prepared by The Museum of Modern Art. Although this is no substitute for screening the film (which *is* necessary with a text like this), it provides a useful examination of the structure of perhaps the most thorough propaganda film ever made.]

Wagnerian marching music.

Blank screen. Then: The eagle, emblem of the German Reich. Swastika.

Titles: Triumph of the Will

> The documentary film of the Reichs-Party Meeting 1934 at Nuremberg.
>
> Produced by the Fuehrer's order.
>
> Created by Leni Riefenstahl.
>
> September 5, 1934. 20 years after the outbreak of World War, 16 years after German woe and sorrow began, 19 months after the commencement of German renascence, Adolf Hitler flew to Nuremberg again, to review the columns of his faithful adherents. (end titles)

Body of film:

An airplane, clouds, bird's-eye view of Nuremberg, of marching columns of Nazi storm troops. Music: *Horst Wessel* song.

---

1. David Stewart Hull, *Film in The Third Reich* (Berkeley: University of California Press, 1969), p. 75.

Reception at aerodrome—cheering women and children. The door of the plane is opened. Hitler steps down, greets with military abruptness. Sees cheering crowds. Grave smile.

Hitler's car rolling through streets, between two rows of cheering crowds. Right arm lifted in right angle, set smile. Behind Hitler's car columns with men in various uniforms. The car rolls past famous buildings of medieval architecture. The car stops. A little girl, sitting on her mother's arm, offers some flowers to the Fuehrer, then lifts arm in Hitler salute. Faces of awed and smiling children. Cheers, cries. High narrow roofs.

Hitler standing erect in his car. His left hand which holds his cap is put against the windscreen of the car. Uniformed orderlies surround the car. Soldiers with steel helmets standing to attention. Hitler, nodding, smiling, steps out. He enters the Hotel Deutscher Hôf. The crowd cheers. Groups of chorus-speakers shouting "Heil Hitler" and "We want to see our leader."

Hitler standing at the window of his hotel room. He lifts his right arm to greet the cheering masses. He looks as if deeply moved. The screen is darkened.

Music, torch-light parade. Drums. The Flag of the German Reich. A serenade is being performed by a military band. Thick crowds of listeners are being gently pushed back by orderlies. The words "Heil Hitler" formed by electric bulbs, the silhouettes of soldiers in helmets are visible in the darkness. Music: military marching songs.

Dawn. Roofs. A window is being opened, a big swastika flag is flying in front of it. Innumerable flags and banners, hanging from the houses are seen flying in the morning wind. A view of the river Pegnitz and its arched bridges. The water, reflecting all these flags. Spires, towers. Chimes. *Meistersinger* music.

Bird's-eye view of rows of white tents. The music is changing into a reveille. Hitler Youth boys beating drums, blowing trumpets. Morning toilet in the open. Showers, laughter, noise. Campfire music. Youths pushing a wagon laden with wood to the field-kitchen for firing. Sausages, beans, soup in large dishes and bowls. Smiling lads crowding around the cook and his helpers for their morning rations of food. Camping Hitler Youth lads wrestling, racing; onlookers; a boy writing a postcard in front of his tent.

Concertina sounds. A man in peasant-costume carrying and playing a concertina, behind him a group of men, women and children in peasant costumes of various German districts: Franconian, Bavarian, Schwalm, Black-Forest costumes.

Hitler, reviewing the peasant group, is striding towards them. He holds out his hand to a woman in peasant costume. She is smiling up to him. He shakes hands with a young girl who beams at him and offers him flowers. Children and young girls are eagerly smiling at him. Handshakes, smiles, cheers.

Music: *Horst Wessel Lied.*[2] Flag-carriers, their profiles turned towards Hitler, parading past him. They stand to attention. Hitler stops to speak or to

---

2. The *Horst Wessel* song was the official battle-song of the National Socialist Party. In English the text would be: "Let's raise our flag, close our ranks, storm troops

shake hands with each of them. Affable, fatherly smile. Grave nods. He steps into his car. Growing, frenzied cheers. Hess acknowledging cheers with Hitler salute.

Interior of large dark hall. Emblem of the Reichs Eagle against banners and curtains, forming the background of a tribune. Meeting. Hess in uniform, speaking on platform:

"I am opening this, our sixth party congress, in respectful remembrance of our General Field-Marshal and Reichspresident von Hindenburg [the audience rises from the seats] who has passed on into eternity. We wish to remember the great Field-Marshal as the first soldier of the Great War, and by this, we are, at the same time, honoring our dead comrades.

"I wish to welcome the high representatives of foreign countries [close-ups of some foreign representatives] who are honoring the party by their presence, and, in sincere friendship, the representatives of our military forces, now under the leadership of our Fuehrer." Waves of applause. Hess, turning to Hitler, slowly as if worshipping:

"My Leader! Around you are gathered the flags and banners of this National Socialism. Their cloth will be threadbare when, looking back, people will be able to understand the greatness of this time and to conceive what you, oh Fuehrer, mean to Germany. You *are* Germany."

Hitler, stern and composed, is looking into the audience. Hess beamingly continues:

"When you are acting, the nation acts. When you are passing judgment, it is the German people that passes judgment. [Cheers] Our Thanks offering is our vow to stand by you for better and for worse, come what may!" Pause. Hess continuing:

"Thanks to your leadership, Germany will attain her aim to be the homeland of all the Germans of the world. [Wild applause] You have been the guarantor of our victory, you are our guarantor of peace." He steps back. Then shouts: "Heil Hitler, Victory Heil." Loud cheers and cries of "Heil Victory." Hess with uplifted right arm faces Hitler. Then Hitler shakes hands with him. Cheers, applause.

Excerpt from the Fuehrer's proclamation, read to the audience by Wagner:

"There is no permanent revolution that would not lead up to anarchy. Just as the world does not live on wars, the nations do not live on revolutions. Nothing great on this earth, lasting and dominating for milleniums, has been built up in decades. The higher a tree, the longer the time of its growth. Things that have to bear up against centuries can grow strong only during centuries."

Rosenberg speaks: "We trust in our young generation that will march on, destined to continue the work which was founded in the stormy years of the Munich revolt and which today is incarnated by the entire nation."

---

march on with firmly-quiet steps. The shadows of the comrades killed by red-front and reactions are marching in our midst."

Dietrich speaks: "Truth is the foundation on which the power of the Press stands and falls, and our only demand to the foreign press is to report the truth about Germany." Applause.

Todt speaks: "The construction of the automobile road system of the Reich has been started in 51 places. Although this is just the beginning, 52,000 men are already working at the construction of this road and another 100,000 men are occupied in the timber-yard, in the quarries, in the bridge-works."

Reinhardt: "Wherever we look, buildings go up everywhere. Everywhere values are being improved or newly created. Active life everywhere since last year and active life will continue in the future."

Darré (peasant-leader): "The health and welfare of the German peasant is the mainstay of internal and export trade and the foundation for prosperity in industry and economic life."

Streicher: "A people that does not attribute the highest value to racial purity must perish."

Ley: "One thought must dominate all our works: to make the worker a proud, upright and equal member of the nation."

Frank: "As head of German justice, all I can say is that for us our supreme leader also represents our supreme judge, and that we know that the principles of justice are sacred to our leader. Therefore, we can assure you that this National Socialist state is a bulwark of freedom and iron justice." Cheers.

Goebbels, with quick smile to the audience, then grave: "May the shining flame of our enthusiasm never be extinguished. This flame alone gives light and warmth to the creative art of modern political propaganda. Rising from the depth of the people, this art must always descend back to it, and find its power there. Power based on guns may be a good thing; it is, however, better and more gratifying to win the heart of a people and to keep it."

Hierl (Head of Labor-Front): "Today the German people has reached the psychic and mental maturity for the introduction of general labor-service conscription. We are waiting for the orders of our leader. Heil!"

Close-up of labor-front flag, bearing the emblem of spade and ear. Music, trumpets, horns.

Hitler is stepping forward on the platform. He salutes, shouting: "Heil, labor-men!"

Hierl continuing: "My Leader! 52,000 laborers are ready for your orders." Continued cheers and "Heil" cries.

A column of uniformed laborers is saluting Hitler with their spades. Drums, melodramatic music.

A chorus of uniformed labor-frontmen "From Silesia," led by a speaker. Chorus: "Here we stand, ready to step into the new era, into Germany."

Speaker: "Comrade, whence dost thou come?" One labor-man: "From Frisia." Speaker: "And thou?" "From Bavaria." "And thou?" "From Koenigsberg" "From Silesia" "From the Black Forest" "From the Rhine" "From the Danube" [pause] "and from the Sarre river."

Chorus: "One people, one leader, one realm, Germany! Today, united in work, we are in the quarries, in the sands, on the dikes of the North Sea. We are planting trees, large forests. We are building roads from village to village, from town to town. New fields we are gaining for the peasant. Forests, corn and bread—for Germany." Close-up of Hitler's profile. Trumpets. Drums.

Speaker and chorus singing: "We are the men of peasant-stock, faithful to our soil!" Drums.

Speaker: "We were not standing in the trenches nor were we under fire, and yet we are soldiers! We are the young people of this realm." Music, playing *I Had A Comrade*. Banners, held by young men in labor-front uniform, are being lowered in memoriam of famous battlefields of the World War.

Speaker: "At Tannenberg, at Verdun, at Liège." Each time the name of a place is pronounced, one banner is laid down. All stand to attention. "At the Somme river, in Flanders, in the West, in the East, in the South, on the seas, on land, and in the skies. Comrades!—shot dead by the reds and reactionaries [the flags are suddenly lifted], you are alive, in Germany!" Emotional silence. Close-up of Hitler, who in grave silence is looking at the various groups. He speaks:

"My labor-servicemen! It is the first time that you are standing here in this formation for review, under my eyes and thus under the eyes of the German people. You represent a great idea. We know that to millions of our people work will be a notion uniting all of them, and, particularly, that there will be no man living in Germany who will see something inferior in the work of the fist [manual labor] as compared to any other work. The whole nation will have to undergo your training. There will be a time at which no German will be able to grow into the community of the people unless he has been in *your* community first. In this hour, not only the hundreds of thousands at Nuremberg but the entire German realm is looking at you. And I know: just as you are serving this German realm in powerful devotion, Germany, in proud joy, will see you, her sons, marching!"

Music. Cannon-shots. The columns sing *We Are Work's Soldiers.* They are marching away.

Marching music. Torches. Silhouettes of stormtroopers in the dark. Cries of "Heil, Victory!" One storm-trooper officer, his profile visible, speaks to the storm-troops:

"Comrades! I remember the time when, in the first years of our movement, I marched as a stormtrooper with you in closed ranks. You stormtroopers have always known one thing only: Service for the Fuehrer!"

Acclamation. Cries of "Heil" and "We want our leader!" Music. Rockets in the darkness. Torchlight fire burning on a tribune. Silhouettes of stormtroopers, looking at the rockets.

Close-up of the mouth of a trumpet, of a drum. Flutes and fifes, played by youngsters of the Hitler Youth formation. Hitler comes. The boys cheer wildly. Hitler smiles and greets, his right hand lifted up in a right angle. He looks pleasantly touched. Hess, at his side, smiles. Hands, flags, cheers. Goebbels eyes the scene through his field-glasses. Hitler salutes the crowds. Hess and Schirach, leader of the Hitler Youth formations, are at his side.

Baldur von Schirach: "My leader, my comrades! Again the hour has come that makes us happy and proud. At your order, my leader, German youth is facing you—a young generation, that does not know notions like class and caste. Because you are the highest expression of unselfishness of this nation, this young generation wants to be unselfish too. Because you are the incarnation of faith for us, we too want to be faithful. Adolf Hitler, the leader of German youth, will speak."

Wild cheers and "Heil" cries. Hitler acknowledges this ovation by emphatic nods. He speaks:

"My German Youth! After one year I can welcome you here again. You are here again, in this shell a section only of what, outside of it, is spread all over Germany. We wish that you German boys and girls absorb in your minds all that we expect of Germany in times to come. We want to be one people and you, my German youth, are to become this people. In the future, we do not wish to see classes and tribes and you must not allow them to develop among you. We want to see one realm in days to come, and we must prepare for this time. We wish this people to be obedient, and you have to practise obedience. We wish this people to be peaceloving but also brave, and you will have to be peaceloving. [Cheers, profile of Hitler in inner emotion] You will have to be peaceloving and, at the same time, courageous. We wish to have no weaklings in this people, and you will have to harden yourselves for this task while you are young. You must learn to bear dangers without ever breaking down. For, whatever you do, we shall pass away, but in *you,* Germany will live on, and when nothing will be left of us, then you will have to hold the banner which we have lifted out of nothingness." He pauses.

"For you are flesh of our flesh, blood of our blood, and in your brain the same spirit which dominates us is at work. Only tied to us can you exist. And when the great columns will march victoriously through Germany, then I know you will join these columns. [Applause] And we know: Germany is within ourselves, Germany is marching in us, and Germany is coming behind us." Among ovations, Hitler is shaking hands with Schirach.

Hitler standing erect in his car—waves, nods, salutes. The youths cheer him, stretching out their right arms. "Heil the leader" cries. Marching music. The car is passing between two rows of Hitler Youth formations who are giving the Nazi salute.

Flags. Profiles of Hitler and his suite. Hitler reviewing cavalry riding past him. Goering and a military dignitary next to him. Parade, tanks, mechanized forces, artillery troops. Cavalry music.

Clouds. Close-up of the Reichs Eagle. A forest of flags, bearing the swastika emblem, carried by invisible hands, seems to be marching. Floodlights at back, lightening the scene. Illuminated platform. Hitler standing on it salutes the flags with outstretched arm. He speaks:

"One year ago, the first meeting of the political leaders of the National Socialist Party took place on this field. Now, 200,000 men have assembled here, summoned by nothing but the order of their hearts, nothing but the commands of faithfulness. Our people's great distress seized us, united us in battle and made us fight and get strong. Therefore, all those who have not suffered the same misery among their own people are unable to understand us. To them it seems a mysterious and incomprehensible thing that has led together hundreds of thousands and made them bear misery, suffering and privation. They think such a thing possible only at the order of the State. They are mistaken. It is not the State that orders us, but we that order the State. [Cheers, applause] It is not the State that has created us, but we that are creating our State." ["Heil" cries]

"Heil our movement! It lives, built on sound foundations and, up to the last breath, each of us will devote his entire strength to the movement, just as in the years gone. Drum to drum, banner to banner, guest to guest. Then, at last, this gigantic column of the united nation will lead together the people which had been disrupted and torn in the past. It would be a crime if we ever gave up what had to be achieved by so much labor, sorrows and sacrifices. [pause] You cannot be unfaithful to something that has given sense and meaning to your whole existence. All this would not be worthwhile, were it not directed by a great command. No earthly being has given us this command, but our Lord, who has created us. Therefore, let us take a vow this evening, namely, at every hour, on each day, to think of Germany, of the nation, of the realm, of our German people. To our German people—Heil Victory, Heil Victory, Heil Victory!"

Cheers, black silhouette of the platform, lights, torches. Fifes, marching feet, hands holding torches: Hitler, right arm raised, is reviewing the parade. Emotional expression.

Reichs Eagle emblem. Open field with two rows of uniformed men seen from bird's-eye view. Broad white road between the rows. Three figures: Hitler, Himmler and *aide de camp* approaching pillar with wreath and flag lying on it. Commemoration of dead party members. Stopping short with outstretched right arms, they step back. Solemn music changing into *I Had A Comrade* tune. Flags are lowered. Fanfares. Officers of elite stormtroop formations, carrying banners, are marching towards the platform on which Hitler is standing. Marching forest of flags. Hitler, with crossed arms and dressed in stormtrooper blouse and breeches, looking on. Military banners, adorned with oakleaves. Drumbeaters. All stand still. Trumpet sounds. One of the officers with banner says:

"My leader! As in old times, when we did our duty, we shall also in future times wait solely for your orders. And we comrades-in-arms know only one thing: to execute the order of our leader. Our leader—Adolf Hitler, Victory Heil!" Crowd cheers.

Hitler speaks: "Men of the storm detachments and troops! A few months ago a dark shadow has spread over our movement. Neither the storm-troops nor any other institution of the party has anything to do with this shadow. All those are mistaken who believe that even the slightest trace of it has crept into our movement. And if anyone is sinning against the spirit of my storm-troops, this will not break the storm-troops but those who dare wrong my faithful ones."

Wild cheers. Hitler lifting his hand as if conducting an orchestra, in an effort to conduct the cheers: "Only a madman or deliberate liar can come to the conclusion that I or one of the others would dissolve what you have built up in many long years. No, comrades, we are firmly standing by this Germany, and we have to stand firmly by her.

"I trust you with the storm-banner, in the conviction that I am bestowing it on the most faithful hands that exist in Germany. For in days gone you have given thousandfold proof of your faith, and in the days to come it cannot be different, and it will not be different. ["Heil"-exclamations] And so I greet you, my old and faithful stormtroopers. Victory Heil, Victory Heil, Victory Heil."

Cannon-shots. Hitler inaugurates banners by touching them with the old battle flag of the party. He shakes hands with each flag-carrier. He looks grim and martial. *Horst Wessel* song is played.

Meistersinger music. Flags. Streets. Hitler in his car. Streets hemmed in with cheering crowds, chiefly women. Decorated windows. People waving hands and small flags at windows. Hitler greets them with smiles and raised right hand. Noise, cheers.

Drums. Goose-stepping Elite troops marching past Hitler. Parade. High naval Officer salutes Hitler. Hitler and Goering, both wearing storm-trooper uniforms, salute. Hess. Reichs-labor-front detachments marching by, saluting the three men. A family looks out of the window of a medieval, flower-and-flag decorated house. Hitler with crossed arms, looking to right and left. Hitler raises his right arm. Close-ups of Ley and Hitler, profile-view.

Storm-troop officers marching past. Parade of military forces. Goose-stepping columns. Hitler salutes them. Motorized forces. People on wooden galleries rise from their seats.

The river Pegnitz reflecting the marching columns. Banner carriers. Nuremberg churches, roofs, monuments. Officers, labor-front men. Front view of Hitler saluting. People looking down from windows. City-gates. Vista of city-gates with leaving troops marching through.

Storm-troop bodyguards. Black Corps (Elite Guard) on parade. Himmler marching ahead of them. Handshake with Hitler. Crowds of spectators. Drummers of storm-troop formations. Goose-stepping stormtroopers. Reichs Eagle. Hitler in back and front view. Hess behind him, walking up to platform in large hall. Hitler and Hess greet audience with smiles. Hitler smiling, perspiring. Applause. Hall decorated with banners and flags. Music: Wagner's *Siegfried* motif. Giant swastika, banners, forming background of platform. Hess stepping forward on platform, says:

"The leader speaks." Frenzied applause. Hitler, immobile, waits for the noise to die down. He clears his throat, then starts:

"The sixth party-meeting of our movement is coming to its close. What may have been but an impressive spectacle, a display of political power for millions of Germans who are not in our ranks, has meant inexpressibly more to the thousands of fighters: the meeting of the old comrades-in-arms!—and perhaps one or the other among you, in spite of the compelling greatness of this troop-review of our party, may have thought back with some wistfulness to those days when it was not an easy thing to be a National Socialist." Pause, applause.

Gesticulating with his right hand: "When our party consisted of only seven men, it already voiced two principles, the first being that this should be a true people's party and the second that it should be the sole and only power in Germany.

"As a party we had to remain a minority, because, at all times, the most valuable elements of fighting and sacrifice have been those who, in the nation, were in the minority, not in the majority. And because these men, the best of the German nation, claimed the leadership of the realm in proud knowledge of their own value, with pride and courage, the people in large numbers have accepted this leadership and supported it." Holding both arms to his sides, he pauses. Close-up chrysanthemums at the right of platform and Hitler.

Continuing with diplomatic, man-of-the-world gestures, raising his left hand: "The German people is happy to know that the eternally changing phases of events have now been definitely replaced by a resting pole." These words are accompanied by wave-like movements of both hands.

With clenched fist: "At all times, only one part of the people will consist of really active fighters. The demands upon them are heavier than those upon the millions of comrades. Mere acceptance is not enough for them. Their motto is: 'I fight.' "

Prolonged cheering. Pointing with his right hand into his audience: "For all times the party will represent the political leading elite of the German people. Unchangeable in its doctrine, hard as steel in its organization, supple and adaptable in its tactics, in its entity, however, a stronghold."

Moving his clenched fist up and down: "All decent Germans are National Socialists. Only the best National Socialists are party comrades." "Heil" cries. Hitler is pausing with arms akimbo.

With contemptuous voice and gestures: "In the past our enemies took care of sifting the chaff from the wheat by waves of prohibition and persecution. Today, *we* must do the mustering and eliminate those who have proved bad and therefore do not belong to us." Accompanied by abrupt gesture, as if tossing off something.

Putting right hand on his heart: "It is our wish and our will that this State and this realm may last in the milleniums to come. [Close-up of soldiers in helmets] We may be happy in the knowledge that this future is entirely ours!"

Opening his arms with rapt gesture: "While the older generation may still be unstable, the young generation is ours, body and soul." In deep emotion, raising his hands in visionary gesture and finally placing them upon his heart: "Only if we are able to make the party the highest embodiment of National Socialist thought and spirit, this party will be an eternal and indestructible pillar of the German people and of our realm. Then our magnificent, glorious army will enter the service of the party which then will be steadied by its tradition, and these two will educate the German people and carry on their shoulders the German State, the German realm!"

With clipped, military voice and gestures: "At this hour, many of our party-members are already leaving this town. And while many of them will still be revelling in recollections of these days, others will be busy already to prepare the next meeting. And again people will come and go, and again they will be moved and inspired, for our ideal and our movement are the living expression of our people, and therefore [moving clenched fist up and down] Heil to the National Socialist movement, Heil to Germany." Continuous, roaring "Heil" cries in the audience. Goering nods his head in agreement, apparently overcome by emotion. Hess looks rapt and solemn, also Hitler. Hess tries to speak but has to wait for the cheering to die down, then says:

"The party is Hitler; Hitler, however, is Germany, just as Germany is Hitler. Hitler Heil! Heil Victory, Heil Victory, Heil Victory."

The *Horst Wessel* song is played. All rise from their seats and join in the singing. Goering, amid the others, seen singing the *Horst Wessel* song. Outstretched right arms, rapt faces.

Gigantic swastika. Marching columns under clouds.

The Nature of Propaganda

John Grierson
(1942)

[Before concluding this section, we should take stock of the moral aspects of the propaganda films—particularly those of the Soviets and the Nazis. The distinguished film-maker and expert on the documentary film, John Grierson, wrote, in 1942, a detailed critique of the Nazis' abuse of cinematic propaganda, offering alternatives to it for Britain and America. Although he applies his critique only to the Nazis, as you read it, see if it has any application to the Soviet use of the medium.]

Long before the war started, those who had studied the development of propaganda were constantly warning the British Government that a highly organized Information Service, national and international, equipped with all modern instruments, was as necessary as any other line of defence. I am thinking back to 1930 and even before Hitler came to power. Over the dog days of the thirties they preached and they pleaded, with only the most partial success; and in the meantime the greatest master of scientific propaganda in our time came up. I don't mean Goebbels: I mean Hitler himself. In this particular line of defence called propaganda, we were caught bending as in so many other spheres, because peace was so much in people's hearts that they would not prepare the desperate weapons of war.

The Germans attached first importance to propaganda. They didn't think of it as just an auxiliary in political management, and military strategy. They regarded it as the very first and most vital weapon in political management and military achievement—the very first. All of us now appreciate how the strategy of position—the war of trenches—was blown to smithereens by the development of the internal combustion engine. Fast-moving tanks and fast troop carriers could get behind the lines. Aeroplanes and flying artillery could get behind the lines. War, in one of its essentials, has become a matter of getting behind the lines and confusing and dividing the enemy.

But the chief way of getting behind the lines and confusing and dividing the enemy has been the psychological way. Hitler was cocksure that France would fall and forecast it in 1934, almost exactly as it happened. The forecast was based on psychological not on military reasons. "France," he said, "in spite of her magnificent army could, by the provocation of unrest and disunity in public opinion, easily be brought to the point when she would only be able to use her army too late or not at all."

The theory behind all this is very simple. Men today, by reason of the great spread of education, are, in part at least, thinking beings. They have been encouraged in individual judgment by a liberal era. They have their own sentiments, loyalties, ideas and ideals; and these, for better or worse, determine their actions. They cannot be considered automata. If their mental and emotional loyalties are not engaged in the cause you present, if they are not lifted up and carried forward, they will fall down on you sooner or later when it comes to total war. The usual way of expressing it is to say that their morale will break.

That is why Hitler said: "It is not arms that decide, but the men behind them—always"; or again, "Why should I demoralize the enemy by military means, if I can do so better or more cheaply in other ways?"; or again, "The place of artillery preparation and frontal attack by the infantry in trench warfare will in future be taken by propaganda; to break down the enemy psychologically before the armies begin to function at all . . . mental confusion, contradiction of feeling, indecisiveness, panic; these are our weapons. When the enemy is demoralized from within, when he stands on the brink of revolution, when social unrest threatens, that is the right moment. A single blow will destroy him."

Just before they entered Norway, the Germans arranged for the State dignitaries in Oslo a special showing of their film of the Polish campaign.[1] A

---

1. *Baptism of Fire.*

portion of that film was included at the end of the American film *The Ramparts We Watch.* Even a portion of the film gave some idea of the effect such a demonstration was likely to have on the peace-loving Norwegians. It showed the mass mechanical efficiency of German warfare with brutal candour. The roaring aeroplanes, the bursting bombs, the flame-throwers, the swift unending passage of mechanized might all constituted an image of the inevitable.

That is how the strategy of terror works. It worked with us in Britain at the time of Munich. I won't say the men had the wind up—in fact I should describe the male reaction as one of vast disappointment and even shame—but the women were weeping all over the place. The picture of inevitable death and destruction Germany wished to present had been successfully presented; and it is one of the best evidences of British stamina that the new united courage of the British people was welded so soon out of these disturbed and doubtful beginnings.

Terror is only one aspect of propaganda on the offensive. The thing works much more subtly than that. Here is a quotation from someone in Hitler's entourage to show how deadly the approach can be: "Every state can, by suitable methods, be so split from within that little strength is required to break it down. Everywhere there are groups that desire independence, whether national or economic or merely political. The scramble for personal advantage and distorted ambition: these are the unfailing means to a revolutionary weapon by which the enemy is struck from the rear. Finally, there are the business men, whose profits are their all in all. There is no patriotism that can hold out against all temptations. It is not difficult to find patriotic slogans that can cover all such enterprises."

We saw in France how groups of men could, in the name of their country, give in to Hitler. Perhaps, in the name of France, they wished to crush the popular front and keep out socialism but they gave in to Hitler. Perhaps, in the name of France, they wanted to crush capitalism in the name of socialism, but they gave in to Hitler. Perhaps, in the name of France, they sighed for some neo-medieval religious authoritarianism but they gave in to Hitler.

In the United States the German inspired organizations did not trade as such. They were always to be found under the slogan "America first" and other banners of patriotism.

The principal point to take is that, when the Germans put propaganda on the offensive in war, their psychological opportunities were rich and widespread. They appealed to men's thwarted ambitions; they offered salvation to disappointed and disheartened minorities; they preyed on the fears of capitalist groups regarding socialism; they preached controlled capitalism and a socialist state to the socialist minded. They harped on those weaknesses of democracy of which democratic citizens are only too well aware; the verbiage of its parliamentary debates, the everlasting delays of its committees, the petty bourgeois ineffectiveness of its bureaucracy. They probed the doubts in the mind of democracy and inflamed them to scepticism. Everything was grist to their mill, so long as they divided the enemy and weakened his belief in himself. No one will say that German propaganda did not do that job brilliantly and well, as it marched its way across Europe. It found the population divided against itself and ready for the knife, and Lavals and Quislings everywhere drilled and rehearsed perfectly in the act of capitulation.

The Germans believed that Democracy had no genuine convictions for which people would be willing to stake their lives. They proceeded cynically on that assumption, marched on that assumption and their entire military plan depended on that assumption. Hanfstaengel actually declared at one time that this lack of conviction within democracy was Hitler's fundamental discovery— "the discovery which formed the starting point for his great and daring policies."

It is perhaps as well that we know where the heart of the matter lies, for if lack of conviction, as they say, always results in defeatism and defeat, the challenge is plain enough. It behoves us to match conviction with greater conviction and make the psychological strength of the fighting democracies shine before the world. It behoves us to match faith with greater faith and, with every scientific knowledge and device, secure our own psychological lines. If propaganda shows a way by which we can strengthen our conviction and affirm it more aggressively against the threat of an inferior concept of life, we must use it to the full, or we shall be robbing the forces of democracy of a vital weapon for its own security and survival. This is not just an idea: it is a practical issue of modern scientific warfare.

Propaganda on the offensive is, like every weapon of war, a cold-blooded one. Its only moral is that the confusion and defeat of the enemy are the supreme good. In that sense it is a black art and in the hands of the Germans was a diabolical one. But, objectively speaking, you will appreciate that it depends for its success on a deep study of the psychological and political divisions of the enemy and is therefore based on close and scientific analysis. Catch-as-catch-can methods in propaganda can no longer serve against an enemy so thorough.

The more pleasant side of international propaganda is the positive side, where you ingratiate yourself with other countries; where you state your cause, establish alliance in spirit and create world confidence that the issue and the outcome are with you. That was Britain's great task, particularly after the fall of France and particularly in regard to the Americas.

Britain's method derives from her great liberal tradition. She is not, I am afraid, very scientific; but she does believe, out of her liberal tradition, that telling the truth must command goodwill everywhere and, in the long run, defeat the distortions and boastings and blatancies of the enemy. The Germans believe that men are essentially weak; they believe that the mainsprings of action are primarily economic and selfish; they believe that men are more interested in the *élan vitale* than the *élan morale;* and they derive the principles of their propaganda accordingly. The British still believe in the *élan morale* and hope that an appeal to the Platonic principle of justice will triumph.

I won't say Britain tells the whole truth but I think that most detached observers agree that she tells as much of it as she reasonably can. The accent of honesty and forthrightness is her principal suit. You would never find the

B.B.C.–you certainly would never find Winston Churchill–under-rating the dangers and difficulties which beset the country. Germany could not get out of her make-up an element of boasting; and Mussolini, for many years, was the image of braggadocio. The British quality, and it has the mark of a national talent, is under-statement; and in the long run–if there is a long run–it is strangely penetrating and effective.

If Britain has a fault, it is that she is still the proud old nation, so sure of her cause and of her good spirit that she takes it too much for granted that other nations will immediately recognize them. You remember what we used to say about English salesmanship. The English said in effect: "Our articles are articles of quality; they have the best craftsmanship in the world behind them and, word of an Englishman, you can take our word for it." It was all very true, but down in South America and elsewhere there were other habits of mind and other habits of buying and the Englishman never quite got round to studying the other fellow's point of view and the special requirements of the market. He certainly never quite got round to saying "The client is always right."

Propaganda, some of us believe, is like selling or showmanship, a study in relativity. I don't mean that it must always, like the chameleon, take its colour from the country or the community in which it is operating. It was the German style to be, cynically, all things to all men, and that was the essence of the German doctrine; but it is not the British. At the same time, a study of the other fellow's point of view is essential.

We used to argue a good deal in pre-war England about the policy of the British Council for Cultural Relations Abroad. There were two schools of thought. One school had not yet got away from the idea that the one way to present Britain abroad was to show the Horse Guards Parade and the ceremonies of old England, Oxford and the law courts, Ascot and Canterbury, the green lawns of the cathedral towns and the lovely rustic quiet of the shires. It was difficult to quarrel with things so fine; but others said plainly: "No, there is a world without, which wants to know more than that. You have a responsibility before the world, in terms of modern leadership, modern ideas and modern achievements. The world wants to know how up-to-date and forward looking you are. It wants to see the light of the future in your eyes as well as the strength and dignity of your past. It wants to know what you are doing to deserve your privileged position in the world; and God keep you if you do not answer them."

If you examine British propaganda today, you will find that there are still the two schools of thought, but I am glad to say that the younger school has been winning hands down. Never, in a sense, was Britain a more modern, revitalized, forward-looking country than she is today.

Britain is beginning to see that accents and styles count in propaganda and that every country has its own way of thinking and its own special focus of interest. "Other nations," says Wickham Steed, "are not interested to hear what good people we are or how excellent our intentions may be. They are interested in what is going to happen to themselves and it should be the business of our propaganda to make this clear to them."

On this question of international differences, I received a letter from England from someone who had seen our Canadian films. He said, was it possible that Canadians thought faster than Englishmen. I replied that when it is a problem of thinking in a straight line, Canadians think much faster; but that when it comes to thinking in five concentric circles, the Englishmen are un-doubtedly the better. Our policy, however, when we send Canadian films abroad is to invite the countries receiving them to remake them in their own style and use their own editorial comment. It sounds curious but there are really vast differences of mental approach as between Canada and England. There is even a vast difference of approach as between New Zealand and Australia. He is a very optimistic propagandist who thinks he can easily pen a message or strike a style which can be called international.

London Can Take It was a beautiful film but it raises a very special issue of relativity in propaganda. That is the difference between primary effects and secondary effects. You might call it the difference between conscious and subconscious effects. *London Can Take It* created enormous sympathy for England and so far so good. The question is whether creating sympathy neces-sarily creates confidence. I cite that psychological problem only to indicate that in the art of propaganda many deep considerations have to be taken into account. Short-range results are not necessarily long-range successes. Conscious effects may not necessarily engage the deeper loyalties of the subconscious. In propaganda you may all too easily be here today and gone tomorrow.

All in all, however, one may be proud of many things in Britain's Information Service. It has followed its own native light and no one will say it has not been a noble light. It has not been scientific, but neither has it been cynical. To its scientific critics it has said with Sir Philip Sidney "If you will only look in thy heart and write, all will be well." I am of the scientific school myself and would leave less to chance in a hard and highly mobilized world. But no one will deny that at least half the art of propaganda lies in the ultimate truth that truth will ultimately conquer.

For myself, I watched the German procedure and wished a little some-times that we could, without running over into harshness and blatancy, say a little more about ourselves and put our propaganda more plainly on the of-fensive. They flooded the world with pictures of action, of their young troops on the march and going places, of deeds done. In their pictures to America, they laid a special emphasis on youth and efficiency and, to people starved of belief in the future, they drummed away with their idea of a new world order. They most subtly showed great respect in their presentation of their French and English prisoners of war and emphasized the model discipline of their troops in occupied territories. They most carefully presented the Führer as a gentle and simple soul, weeping over his wounded soldiers, kind to children, humble in his triumphs. It was a calculated, impressive, positive picture as they presented it.

The Germans' careful study of the requirements of particular countries must have had particular effect in South America. They appreciated the South American objection to being exploited by alien capital and posed carefully as the outside friend who wished nothing so much as to help them be themselves and develop themselves. They knew how to pump in free news services to countries which appreciated them—by radio from Berlin, translated and typed out and put pronto on the editorial desk by local German agents. On the special national days of these countries to the south they knew how to shoot flattering broadcasts from Berlin, in the language of the country and with the fullest knowledge of the local vanities to be flattered.

The Germans knew better than to say, as a certain well-known American said of cultural relations with South America, that "the idea was to spread the American idea to the South American Republics." I have no doubt he thought the American idea God's own blessing to mankind, but it is worth remembering that not a few South Americans, allied to a more aristocratic and courtly tradition, still regard the American idea as the ultimate in barbarism—or as a French jester has put it, an idea "which has passed from barbarism to degeneracy without any intervening period of civilization." The Germans certainly knew better than to define their interest in South America with the *naïvete* of an advertisement in *Time*. "Southward," it declared, in a phrase calculated to raise every hackle south of the Rio Grande, "Southward, lies the course of Empire."

Where the Germans failed was in the fact that their cold-blooded cynicism spilled over and was spotted. You can impress other countries with your might and your will. You may even impress them with your new world order. But you can't start blatantly talking of conscience as a chimera; morals as an old wives' tale; the Christian religion as a dream of weaklings; and the pursuit of truth as *bourgeois* fiddle-faddle, without raising a few doubts in the heart of mankind.

Finally, there is propaganda within our gates. I suggested earlier that faith must be met with greater faith and that our first line of defence is in the unity of our purpose in these ideological struggles which are now upon us.

A democracy by its very nature and by its very virtues lies wide open to division and uncertainty. It encourages discussion; it permits free criticism; it opens its arms wide to the preaching of any and every doctrine. It guards jealously this liberty of the individual, for it is of the essence of democracy and, in the long run, makes for justice and civilization. But in times of stress it is difficult to see the wood for the trees. Whilst we are consulting this freedom and that, we may lose that discipline, that centralized power and dynamic, by which the principle of liberty itself is safeguarded from those who are less punctilious. When we are challenged in our philosophy and our way of life, the beginning is not in the word but in the act.

The Nazi viewpoint was that we had not found within our democratic way of life a sufficient dynamic of action to meet their challenge—that it was not in our nature to find it—and that we should not find it. "The opposition," said

Hitler, "is dismally helpless, incapable of acting, because it has lost every vestige of an inner law of action."

In the long run they found that was not true but it would be folly to dismiss this criticism without thinking about it. The self-respect of free men provides the only *lasting* dynamic in human society; and the most powerful and vivid statement of this proposition is to be found in Walt Whitman's preface to his *Leaves of Grass*. But we also know that free men are relatively slow in the uptake in the first days of crisis. We know that much that has become precious to free men in a liberal régime must be forsworn in days of difficulty—the luxury of private possession and private security—the luxury of private deviation in thought and action—the supreme luxury of arguing the loss. Moreover, your individual trained in a liberal régime demands automatically that he be *persuaded* to his sacrifice. It may sound exasperating but he demands as of right—of human right—that he come in only of his own free will.

All this points to the fact that instead of propaganda being less necessary in a democracy, it is more necessary. In the authoritarian state you have powers of compulsion and powers of repression, physical and mental, which in part at least take the place of persuasion. Not so in a democracy. It is your democrat who most needs and demands guidance from his leaders. It is the democratic leader who most must give it. If only for the sake of quick decision and common action, it is democracy for which propaganda is the more urgent necessity.

There is another deep reason for the development of propaganda in a democracy. The educational beliefs of democracy have been criticized. "Universal education," said the Nazis, "is the most corroding and disintegrating poison that liberalism ever invented for its own destruction." This, of course, is another distortion, but there is again a grain of truth. With universal education, democracy has set itself an enormous and an enormously difficult task. We have had it for two or three generations only; and it would be crazy to think that in that short experience we have worked out a perfect technique or discovered all the principles by which it should be guided. Our system of universal education has made vast mistakes and has today grotesque weaknesses. Every progressive educationist knows that. This does not mean that we must throw the essential machinery of democracy into the discard, but rather that we must correct its mistakes and strengthen it where it is now weak.

There are some of us who believe that propaganda is the part of democratic education which the educators forgot; and that is what first attracted us to study its possibilities. Education has always seemed to us to ask too much from people. It has seemed to expect every citizen to know everything about everything all the time—a patent impossibility in a world which grows wider and more complicated every day. We believe that education has concentrated so much on people knowing things that it has not sufficiently taught them to feel things. It has given them facts but has not sufficiently given them faith. It has given them the three R's but has not sufficiently given them that fourth R which is Rooted

Belief. We believe that education in this essential has left men out in the bush without an emotional map to guide them; and when men are starved of belief they are only too prone to believe anything.

If you recall the origin of the word propaganda, you will remember that it was first associated with the defence of a faith and a concept of civilization. Propaganda first appeared in the description of the Catholic office—Congregatio de Propaganda Fide—which was to preach and maintain the faith. It may be just as easily today the means by which we preach and maintain our own democratic faith. Man does not live by bread alone, nor the citizen by mind alone. He is a man with vanities to be appealed to, a native pride to be encouraged. He has a gambler's heart to be allowed a flutter and a fighting instinct which can be associated with fighting for the right. One part of him at least asks to live not safely but adventurously.

So we may usefully add a new dramatic factor to public education—an uplifting factor which associates knowledge with pride and private effort with a sense of public purpose. We can, by propaganda, widen the horizons of the schoolroom and give to every individual, each in his place and work, a living conception of the community which he has the privilege to serve. We can take his imagination beyond the boundaries of his community to discover the destiny of his country. We can light up his life with a sense of active citizenship. We can give him a sense of greater reality in the present and a vision of the future. And, so doing, we can make the life of the citizen more ardent and satisfactory to himself.

We can, in short, give him a leadership of the imagination which our democratic education has so far lacked. We can do it by radio and film and a half a dozen other imaginative media; but mostly, I hope, we shall do it by encouraging men to work and fight and serve in common for the public good. To have men participate in action is the best of all propagandas; and radio and films and the rest of them are only auxiliary to that.

Canada is a young nation which has not yet found herself but is today in the exciting process of doing so. I like to think that the breathless reception given to the King and Queen was due not so much to their presence, brilliant as it was, but to the fact that Canada found for the first time a ceremonial opportunity of raising her young national face to the sunlight. I like to think that subconscious Canada is even more important than conscious Canada and that there is growing up swiftly in this country, under the surface, the sense of a great future and of a great separate destiny—as Canada.

In other words, I believe the country is ripe, if its imagination is given true leadership, for a new burst of energy and a new expression of Canada's faith in herself. In these circumstances, I don't think it would be difficult to create a powerful sense of spiritual unity, whatever the threat may be.

FOR DISCUSSION

1. In an article on the Soviet cinema written in 1930, Sergei Eisenstein cited all of the advantages he saw in a socialist film industry which was not motivated by private profits. He argued in favor of a state-controlled motion picture industry to meet "popular needs." What does he mean by this claim? Can an artist be creative under rigorous state-domination? Under state control is it possible for a film-maker to produce any work which is not propaganda? As you read about American film production (which is privately controlled) in the next section, consider what pressures private control and profit-making put on the film-maker.

2. Based on Timothy Angus Jones's summary-outline of *Potemkin* and Warshow's criticism of the work of the Soviet film-makers (and hopefully after screening several Soviet films), consider the following questions:

(a) Is there anything democratic in the viewpoints of such films? Can an audience reach its conclusion about the films' subject matter after screening them?

(b) Are such films totally manipulative of their audience, or, do they serve a valuable educational role?

(c) What kind of justification can you give for films of a "centralized" ideology? What case can you make against them?

3. It is clear even from the most critical writings in this section that the Soviets and the Nazis made great stylistic contributions to the cinema. Some evaluations have labeled these films great works of art, regardless of their manipulative content. Can films like *Triumph of the Will* be considered "art"? Can propaganda also be "art"? Is art neutral to political dogma? Should it be? Can these films be considered as art outside the societies which produced them? Would you advocate their screening— merely for artistic purposes (for students of style and technique)— regardless of their inflammatory content? Why or why not?

4. Canadian John Grierson's critique of the Nazi manipulation of film implies that Western democracies will never use the medium so diabolically. After reading his essay, use it as a guideline for analyzing the American film propaganda of the World War II era and the Cold War. In this respect, is his faith in Western democracy justified? Discuss.

PART THREE

American Propaganda Films

The American movie industry—Hollywood—was far removed from its Soviet and Nazi counterparts. Privately financed, and designed primarily as an entertainment medium with an eye on popularity and profits, the Hollywood movie has *never* been directly state-manipulated for propaganda purposes. However, in times of national crises—particularly wartime—Hollywood has patriotically directed several of its products toward providing a spirit of national unity. During America's involvement in World War I (1917–18), a number of "America will win" epics, designed to stimulate a unified spirit behind the doughboys, were produced. Such films were, for the most part, inept and absurd, depicting Germans as "savage Huns" and Americans and their allies as saviors of Europe. Probably the most ludicrous of these World War I potboilers was *Why America Will Win,* made by the Fox Company in 1918. This film was supposed to be the biography of America's commanding general, John Pershing. Its relation to reality is illustrated by the press release summary which concluded: "Pershing leads a triumphant march into Berlin and tells the Kaiser what is what. The destruction of Berlin follows . . . the Kaiser is killed by lightning. . . ."

The reviews of the World War I efforts at propaganda reprinted in this section indicate the feebleness of Hollywood's effort. Even the two epics by the noted film genius, D. W. Griffith (*Hearts of the World* and *The Great Love*), were merely extensions of the "kill-the-Hun" genre. Somewhat more realistic were the earliest films made by the U. S. War Department, which used Hollywood technicians, but which were totally separate from the commercial film industry.

During World War II (1939–45), the United States made extensive use of motion pictures as propaganda tools. Unlike the feeble efforts during World War I, the American film industry mobilized itself on several levels to unify Americans in their struggle against Germany and Japan. Generally two types of cinematic propaganda were employed during the war, according to the depth of American involvement:

1. Hollywood Preparedness—films made prior to America's entry into the war (1939–41), designed to quash isolationist sentiments and to stimulate public opinion against Germany.
2. Hollywood at War—films made immediately after America's entry into the war, showing the valor of the U. S. fighting man against the evil "Krauts" and "Japs."

49

WORLD WAR I
War Vividly Seen in Griffith Film
(*The New York Times,* April 5, 1918)

Invited spectators who filled the Forty-fourth Street Theatre last night were stirred as few audiences at war plays and photoplays have been by the private showing of D. W. Griffith's *Hearts of the World,* which will have its first public presentation at the theatre tonight. Mr. Griffith's film seeks to make the war a big reality, to bring as much of it as possible within the four walls of a comfortable Broadway theatre, and, if the demonstrations by which those who saw the picture manifested their succession of emotions can be accepted as faithful indications, the motion picture succeeds in its ambitious aim.

But the picture is not just a series of photographs of fighting. Mr. Griffith does not plunge his spectators straight into action that would be only confusing and spectacular. His story begins some years before the war, the scene in a quiet French village where the homely people have no thought of war and death and disaster. There is a young girl living with her old grandparents. And there is a young man living with his parents and three little brothers. Monsieur Cuckoo, The Little Disturber, The Village Carpenter, A Deaf and Blind Musician, and many others are village characters with their happiness and little difficulties that do not matter.

The Girl and the Boy love each other. The Little Disturber, delightful little devil of a flirt, loves the Boy, but he loves the other Girl and angrily spurns her. The Disturber at last turns to Monsieur Cuckoo, who has been pursuing her from the first. The Littlest Brother of the Boy, as fascinating a little fellow as has been seen on any stage, idolizes his big brother and gives the spectators much amusement with his merry exhibitions of affection. The scenes of this French village suggest all that had been known by travel and books of provincial France before the war. Many times those in the theatre broke into applause just at some particularly beautiful landscape or rural vista.

Into such an atmosphere and environment the war bursts. First a German spy inspecting possible fortifications appears with sinister suggestion. Then, just before the set wedding day of the Boy and the Girl, the town crier startles the village with the mobilization order. The whole peaceful arrangement of life is violently shattered. The men rush off to war and the women stay behind to worry and wonder.

With the beginning of the war, the film introduces the first of the scenes of actual fighting made by Mr. Griffith at the front with the co-operation of the British and French Governments. These scenes are skillfully worked into others specially made for the play, so that, were it not for the appearance of characters peculiar to the plot of the play, one would scarcely know where the actual ends

From the motion picture **Hearts of the World.** Courtesy of Museum of Modern Art.

and the made-to-order begins. Sometimes one does not know whether what he is seeing is a real war or screen make-believe. The pictures of hand to hand fighting in the trenches, the bursting of shells from big guns, the demolition of buildings, the scouting trips and raids into enemy trenches are impressively realistic.

Continuing the story, the Germans advance against the village; many of the inhabitants flee in confusion, while shells do their destruction around them; others remain behind and seek shelter in cellars and crypts and vaults. Certain characters in the play are killed; others survive to face the fearful future. After furious fighting the Germans take possession of the town and Prussian brutality reveals itself in a number of vivid scenes.

The horrors of German occupation are shown, chiefly as they affect the persons in the play, the Girl and the Disturber, who become companions in misery. There is a great deal of detail, both of actual fighting and of play plot, and finally the Boy, whom the girl had left for dead on a battlefield, enters the village disguised in the uniform of a Prussian officer and finds his sweetheart, who escapes with him from the clutches of a Prussian officer to a garret room, where a struggle that has all of the thrill of melodrama takes place. But this little clash of individuals is not long continued. Soon the French troops retake the town and more of the action of real war is seen.

The conclusion shows the characters of the play, lovers reunited on a furlough, and as they are dining, American troops pass outside. The Stars and Stripes enter, and at the very end ultimate victory for the Allies is symbolically forecast.

All of the actors in the play were frequently applauded. Lillian Gish, as the Girl, moved the people in her biggest moments, and Dorothy Gish, as the Little Disturber, with her bewitching ways, was applauded many times after stepping beyond the range of the camera just as if she had been on the stage in person, retreating into the wings after an effective scene. Ben Alexander as the Littlest Brother was a child wonderful, and Robert Harron as the Boy, Robert Anderson as Monsieur Cuckoo, George Fawcett as the Village Carpenter, and Eugene Pouyet as a Poilu were especially good.

Descriptive music, in which the leading characters had motifs that accompanied their appearances, added greatly to the performance.

After "The End" had been flashed upon the screen the spectators stood and shouted for Mr. Griffith until he appeared on the stage. He said that he had no speech to make, but only wanted to thank those present. When he attempted to ask the spectators to pray for and support the men fighting in the war, which, he said, the flickering shadows on the screen represented in a small way, his voice broke and he never finished his sentence.

Historic meetings of the British Parliament and French Chamber of Deputies, as well as the leading figures in France and England, were shown and received ovations. A representation of the Kaiser was eagerly hissed.

The scenario of the play was written by M. Maston de Tolignac and translated by Captain Victor Marier. The film is presented under the management of William Elliott, F. Ray Comstock, and Morris Gest.

Many officers of the allied armies and navies, public officials, and friends of the producers were present by invitation.

Hearts of the World

Kenneth Macgowan

(*The New Republic*, July 20, 1918)

It is a singular and significant fact that twenty years of progress in the movies—progress greater than any other art has shown in a like time—leave the main source of interest just where they found it: How is it all done? When the movies showed us trotting horses and locomotives in motion, we suffered the passion of Budge and Toddie to "see the wheels go round." It is a little disheartening to discover that this is still the only really important reaction when a gigantic and costly film like D. W. Griffith's *Hearts of the World* shows us two or three army divisions, a flock of mammoth cannon and large sections of the Western front given over to arousing our emotion about war-stricken families and the fate of nations, and to demonstrating most effectively the deep animal patriotism which lurks in the most pacific of us. Twenty years ago we wanted to know how they made the trotting horses move. Today we want to know how they make our emotions move. For the unmistakably meretricious effect of almost every story ever screened drives us back to discuss the problem of how the thrill is made.

Hearts of the World—for all its combination of Lloyd George, the ruined town of Ham, and a tremendous emotional sweep—*is* meretricious. The reason might be its obvious story of a Franco-American lover separated from his fiancée by outbreak of the war, and his fight to rescue her from the customary designs of a genuine newspaper Hun. It might be this common, stupid, leaky old tale, if it weren't for the fact that practically every story, however good it may have been in some other medium, seems to leave something of the same effect when really well done on the screen. Perhaps physical narration reduces life to its too crude essentials. Perhaps the tremendous bare emotion of the movies turns us aside. Is the screen the demonstrating laboratory of the new psychology, which poses us as striving to escape from emotion to reason, from importunate desire to sentimental fulfilment, from the physical life to the mental?

At any rate, *Hearts of the World* thrills and sickens beyond measure, and drives us back to a keen interest in how Mr. Griffith does the trick. . . . It is . . . technical matters—possibilities, failures and achievements—that first and finally interest the practised movie-goer who submits himself the the nerve-racking business of sitting through *Hearts of the World*. Curiously enough, they seem more important than this tawdry story built upon a world's terror and deliverance, the sight of France rising to the Marseillaise, and the final staggering moment of the arrival of the American troops in Paris. And yet there is a strange and unescapable fact which does a lot to chasten our interest in Mr. Griffith's technique. Here we have an art of pure emotion which can go beneath thought, beneath belief, beneath ideals, down to the brute fact of emotional psychology, and make a man or a woman who has hated war, all war, even this war, feel the surge of group emotion, group loyalty and group hate. In the face of this power—momentary and passing though it may be—the emotions which this director wants to interpret assume considerable importance, and still more important become the emotions of his own temperament which dictate them. It is just a little disturbing to recollect that Mr. Griffith's films have demonstrated in their maker a vivid, an over-vivid, flair for violence, passion and horror, for child-like and animal devotion, for blood-hot courage and blood-hot desire, but none for the finer and larger qualities of faith and heroism which seem to deserve their place in the movies as well as in life.

One would hardly care to level at the works of Mr. Griffith the accusation Mr. Shaw launched at Shakespeare's: "search for statesmanship, or even citizenship, or any sense of the commonwealth, material or spiritual, and you will not find the making of a decent vestryman or curate in the whole horde. As to faith, hope, courage, conviction, or any of the true heroic qualities, you will find nothing but death made sensational, despair made stage-sublime, sex made romantic, and barrenness covered up by sentimentality and the mechanical lilt of blank verse." But *Hearts of the World,* like *The Birth of a Nation* and *Intolerance,* leaves you feeling as if, in spite of his genius, the man who has led you through these scenes of nerve-rack misses something or other rather vital in the Shavian catalogue of virtues.

WORLD WAR II
Hollywood Preparedness (1939-1941)

The overstated, unsubtle, and often absurd American propaganda films of World War I generally reflected the level of cinematic art of that time. After the War, with the devastating developments in the Soviet and Nazi propaganda machines, and the vast technical innovations in movie making, the cinematic potential for propaganda was more greatly realized in America. With the coming of World War II, launched by Germany's attack on Poland in 1939, the United States (though officially neutral) began to take steps in her foreign policy to aid the enemies of the Nazis. Despite this, however, there was a good deal of isolationist sentiment among the American people, and the nation's film industry, reflecting the new activist internationalism of the government, began to produce a series of commercial movies designed to expose the perils of isolationism in a world threatened by Nazi madness. Although some of the films of this period (1939–41) were cheap potboilers like their World War I counterparts, several were a good deal more complex. Films like Charlie Chaplin's *The Great Dictator, The Mortal Storm,* and The March of Time's *The Ramparts We Watch* skillfully presented the potential dangers of Nazism to Americans—and, at the same time, generated a good deal of controversy among isolationists.

Author John Grierson, whose criticism of Nazi propaganda films was presented earlier, wrote an essay in 1940 (while staying in Hollywood) describing the American film industry's interests in the European war and its potential power as a propaganda medium. Here, Grierson is an advocate of film propaganda. Following Grierson's comments, the remainder of this section is composed of reviews and essays about the most important commercial films which advocated American preparedness prior to entry in World War II. Of particular interest here is the full-length March of Time feature, *The Ramparts We Watch*, which contained a segment of the German compilation film, *Baptism of Fire* (see Part Two). The controversy over *Ramparts* is especially interesting since it raises all sorts of questions about "ethical" propaganda and draws several parallels to the German model which it condemns. Keep this in mind as you read the material concerning it.

The Film at War

John Grierson
(1940)

The day war with Germany broke out, I was in Hollywood. I suppose everyone will remember that day in minute personal detail. It was the same on 4th August 1914. We all sensed, like a cloud on the mind, that here was the end of one epoch, the beginning of another, and all our personal worlds might never be the same again.

On 4th August 1914 I was on the coast of the Scottish Hebrides and the war was very near. I spent the whole day watching the trawlers and the drifters breasting the tide, puffing their way back in hundreds to become minesweepers and anti-submarine patrols. But on 3rd September 1939 I was in Hollywood, 6,000 miles away from the Scottish coast, and the seat of war. No minesweepers or anti-submarine patrols. Only white yachts, gliding along on a smooth blue Pacific. California was sunning itself on the beaches and Hollywood was behind me, the city of unreality, stardust, and people's dreams.

Yet instead of feeling a world away from the war, I felt no distance at all. I knew very well that there beside me in Hollywood was one of the greatest potential munition factories on earth. There, in the vast machinery of film production, of theatres spread across the earth with an audience of a hundred million a week, was one of the great new instruments of war propaganda. It could make people love each other or hate each other. It could keep people to the sticking point of purpose.

And that is how it is in our modern world. Like the radio and the newspaper, the film is one of the keys to men's will, and information is as

Reprinted by permission of Faber and Faber Ltd. and Praeger Publishers, Inc. Copyright Praeger Publishers, Inc., from *Grierson on Documentary*, edited by Forsyth Hardy.

necessary a line of defence as the army, the navy, and the air force. The leaders responsible for the conduct of war have to ask new kinds of questions. Which nation puts its case insistently and well and makes converts and allies? Who arouses the national loyalty? Who makes purpose commanding? Who mobilizes the patrol ships of the human mind? These are vital considerations among statesmen today. In the thirties European politics seemed to turn on the effect of propaganda and every nation was fighting for command of the international ether. Even the issue of the war may turn on the skill and imagination with which we formulate our aims and maintain the spirit.

In the early months of the war the film was mobilized like the newspaper and the radio alongside the fighting forces of the nations. Even Hollywood, far from the battlefront, was immediately affected. I never saw so great a scurry in my life as in that first week of war in the chambers of Hollywood's magnates. A third of their world market had vanished overnight or become completely uncertain. Who knew when the bombs would be raining from the sky and making theatres in the European cities untenable? The black-outs had driven people from the screen romance to sit by their radios for the latest war news.

Hollywood was so nervous that it had a new idea every day. The first reaction was to draw in its economic horns, make cheaper pictures, intensify its American market. There was some talk of forgetting its international role and going all American. The result of that policy was seen in more pictures of North American history, more pictures of South America. Hollywood even began, in a sudden burst of light, to remember that Canada was a North American country.

There was another school of thought in Hollywood which remembered the war of 1914–18 and how the frothier kinds of entertainment had prospered. A great deal was heard in these first days about stopping serious pictures and giving people nothing but light-hearted ones—to permit them to forget their worries. "Give them more fluff" was the way Hollywood described it. But not for long. The more modern school of production, the younger men, argued vehemently in every studio. They said, I think wisely, that people would be asking more questions in this war, and that this policy of froth and fluff would be an insult to the intelligence of the people. I confess I was greatly interested to hear how seriously these younger producers talked—the men like Walter Wanger. There was no question of avoiding world responsibility, no desire whatever to forget the war and make a false paradise of neutrality. In Wanger's office we installed a ticker service from the United Press and daily we sat around it, reading the war news, considering how best the film might serve mankind in this new situation. Everyone in this particular group was for going into propaganda of some kind, but everyone I noticed was for avoiding hatred. No *Beast of Berlin* and other childish exaggerations this time, they said. And through all their thoughts I noticed there ran the theme: "Let us do something to keep the decent human values alive. Let us so maintain men's sanity that when it comes to peace, we shall know how to make it stable."

The warring nations had to be much more direct. They reached out, at once, to make the film their recruiting sergeant. In the newsreels they made the film an instrument of international information by which they could tell the world about their efficiency, their power, their confidence, and their will to win.

That new mood was apparent in two of the first films to come from Britain. There was not much peace in *The Warning*. It was a picture of England preparing for death and disaster; and you saw the old England made grotesque by war as in a distorting mirror. There was no peace in *The Lion Has Wings*. That work of film documentation was Britain actually at war, zooming and roaring above the clouds. It was also the film at war. There would be more and more as the days went on. And they would be far more real, far more documentary, these films of war, than any seen before from British studios.

I have been for a long time interested in propaganda and it is as a propagandist I have been from the first interested in films. I remember coming away from the last war with the very simple notion in my head that somehow we had to make peace exciting, if we were to prevent wars. Simple notion as it is, that has been my propaganda ever since—to make peace exciting. In one form or another I have produced or initiated hundreds of films; yet I think behind every one of them has been that one idea, that the ordinary affairs of people's lives are more dramatic and more vital than all the false excitements you can muster. That has seemed to me something worth spending one's life over.

I should have been an unhappy person if I had thought all this vanished with the war. Strangely enough the war seemed only to accentuate people's hunger for reality. It was proper that the film should take its place in the line of defence, as in duty bound. It was proper that it should use its powers to mobilize the full effort of the nation. But—so it seemed in these early months—one way, too, in which we could maintain our defences and keep our spirit for the struggle ahead was to remember that the aims of our society lie beyond war and in the love of peace. It would be a poor information service, it seemed, which kept harping on war to the exclusion of everything, making our minds narrow and anaemic. It would be a poor propaganda which taught hatred, till it violated the sense of decency which ten thousand years of civilization have established. It would be an inefficient national information which did not keep the home fires of national activity burning, while the men were off to the war. In war as in peace, strength lies in hope, and it is the wisest propaganda which keeps men rich in hope.

The war would have achieved its final feat of destructiveness, and we should have been brought to the very brink of spiritual suicide, if we had lost the sense of what we were defending.

On this serious question of the relation of peace thoughts and war thoughts, I am going to quote from the great French writer, Giraudoux. Addressing the children of France, as Director of the French Ministry of Information, at the opening of their school year, he said:

"Thirty-eight thousand of your teachers have had to take machinegun, bomb, and grenade and all the abhorred tools of destruction to form a rampart behind which you will be sheltered this winter—to learn from the masters left to you—and from your school books—your country's inviolable love of peace. . . . Young sentinels, learn a true history, a true geography, a moral without hatred, lessons in things which have nothing to do with gunpowder and bayonets."

So there you have it. There are two sides to propaganda, and two sides to the film at war. The film can be mobilized to give the news and the story of a great historical event. In that sense our aim was to use it for all its worth to secure the present. But my hope has been that the film would also be used more and more to secure the future and serve the still wider needs of the people of Canada. War films, yes, but more films, too, about the everyday things of life, the values, the ideals which make life worth living. I hoped that we could use the film to give visual significance to the words of the Canadian Prime Minister when he said that the spirit of mutual tolerance and the respect for fundamental rights are the foundation of the national unity of Canada.

In that way I have thought to rescue from these barren days of trouble something we could hand on to the future.

Confessions of a Nazi Spy

Frank S. Nugent
(*The New York Times*, May 29, 1939)

[One of the first Hollywood films to depict the evils of Nazi activity was Warner Brothers' *Confessions of a Nazi Spy* (1939). Though not a very sophisticated exposé (as the *New York Times* review indicates), the film scared the German-American Bund (a pro-Nazi organization) into filing a libel suit against Warner Brothers, charging defamation of character. It is interesting to note that the same studio made a similar film in 1951 exposing Soviet agents in the U.S.—*I Was a Communist for the FBI*. (See reference to that film on p. 117.)]

Confessions of a Nazi Spy, screen play by Milton Krims and John Wexley based on material gathered by Leon G. Turrou; directed by Anatole Litvak for Warner Brothers. At the Strand.

Ed Renard . . . . Edward G. Robinson
Schneider . . . . Francis Lederer
Schlager . . . . George Sanders
Dr. Kassel . . . . Paul Lukas

Attorney Kellogg .... Henry O'Neill
Erika Wolff .... Lya Lys
Mrs. Schneider .... Grace Stafford
Scotland Yard Man .... James Stephenson
Krogman .... Sig Rumann

Hitler's pledge of non-aggression toward the Americas reached the Warners too late yesterday. They had formally declared war on the Nazis at 8:15 A. M. with the first showing of their *Confessions of a Nazi Spy* at the Strand. Hitler won't like it; neither will Goebbels; frankly, we were not too favorably impressed either, although for a different reason. We can endure just so much hissing, even when Der Fuehrer and the Gestapo are its victims. The Warners had courage in making the picture, but we should have preferred to see them pitch their battle on a higher plane.

Based on the evidence presented by the G-men during last year's spy trials and on newspaper gleanings, the film's quasi-documentary character has been supported by its employment of newsreel shots of Hitler haranguing his Brownshirts, a commentator's voice, maps and other factual pictorial matter. But its editorial bias, however justified, has carried it to several childish extremes. Membership in the National Socialist party cannot be restricted entirely to the rat-faced, the brute-browed, the sinister. We don't believe Nazi propaganda Ministers let their mouths twitch evilly whenever they mention our Constitution or Bill of Rights. We thought that school of villainy had gone out with *The Beast of Berlin*, made back in '14.

Since most of the facts are known, it seems superfluous to go into the story at all, except to mention that the Warners, conscious as they are of the spy and propaganda menaces, still are encouragingly confident of America's proof against them both. As Edward (G-man) Robinson remarks, the Nazis must be mad to think they can get away with it. So, after Francis Lederer, Paul Lukas, Dorothy Tree, Joe Sawyer and the other enemy agents have had their comeuppance, the Warners eavesdrop on a couple of the boys in a lunch-wagon and discover that Uncle Sam still is their favorite relative.

As melodrama, the film isn't bad at all. Anatole Litvak has paced it well, and the performances of Mr. Robinson as the Federal man, Mr. Lederer as the weak link in the Nazi spy network and Mr. Lukas as the propaganda agent are thoroughly satisfactory. But the film's promised revelations have long been in the public domain, and we cannot fight down the impression that the picture has cheapened its cause and sacrificed much of its dignity by making its villains twirl their long black mustaches. (A short black one can be villainous enough.)

Warners Ready
to Defend Selves Against Kuhn

(*The New York World,* September 4, 1939)

Warner Brothers Pictures today answered the $5,000,000 libel suit brought by Fritz Kuhn, head of the German-American Bund, by admitting that the picture, *Confessions of a Nazi Spy,* was based upon the activities of the Bund and by stating that they would prove that scenes of spying and perversive activity portrayed there are true.

Demanding the right of a jury trial to prove their allegations, Warners filed what was considered an unusually strong answer to the libel charge. Their attorneys said the picture actually was based upon un-American, Nazi-dictated propaganda, sabotage and treason and based upon the facts disclosed at the spy trials in this city and in the Panama Canal Zone.

The legal document demanded a jury trial so that the anti-democratic tactics of the Bund might be better held up to the light of examination in open court.

The $5,000,000 libel was brought by Kuhn against the picture's producers and against Leon G. Turrou, former G-man, and against Milton Krims and John Wexley, who collaborated with Mr. Turrou on the scenario. All of the defendants were represented by the answer filed by R. W. Perkins, attorney for Warner Brothers.

"This picture is true to life as to technique and method," said the long document, filed today with the clerk of the Federal Court. "It is based upon evidence adduced in the German spy trials here and in Panama that resulted in convictions. We are willing to base our case on the records in those trials."

The Bund and its members, said the answer, "are active militant propagandists of Nazi ideology." It said the Bund "supports and would plant and propagate the undemocratic principles of Adolf Hitler and are therefore disloyal to the United States."

The legal document said the Nazi government organized and fostered the Bund.

"It seeks to promote religious prejudice," the answer said of the Bund. "It advocates destruction of the Constitution and the Bill of Rights. Bund members masquerade as loyal Americans under the protection of citizenship papers, but consider themselves as loyal to Germany."

The Bund, Warner Brothers said, carries the swastika, sings the Horst Wessel song, the hymn of the Nazi party, and receives direct aid from the German government.

Mr. Turrou was chief of the G-men who rounded up Nazi sympathizers and German seamen who were found guilty of spying in plane factories and attempting to gain secret information from the armed services. He resigned after the trial ended and helped produce the picture to which Kuhn objected.[1]

The Mortal Storm

Bosley Crowther
(*The New York Times*, June 21, 1940)

The Mortal Storm; screen play by Claudine West, Andersen Ellis and George Froeschel; based on the novel by Phyllis Bottome; directed by Frank Borzage for Metro-Goldwyn-Mayer. At the Capitol.

Freya Roth	Margaret Sullavan
Martin Breitner	James Stewart
Fritz Marberg	Robert Young
Professor Roth	Frank Morgan
Otto Von Rohn	Robert Stack
Elsa	Bonita Granville
Mrs. Roth	Irene Rich
Erich Von Rohn	William T. Orr
Mrs. Breitner	Maria Ouspenskaya
Rudi	Gene Reynolds
Rector	Russell Hicks
Lehman	William Edmunds
Marta	Esther Dale
Holl	Dan Dailey Jr.
Professor Berg	Granville Bates
Professor Werner	Thomas Ross
Franz	Ward Bond

At last and at a time when the world is more gravely aware than ever of the relentless mass brutality embodied in the Nazi system, Hollywood has turned its camera eye upon the most tragic human drama of our age. In Metro's *The Mortal Storm,* which opened yesterday at the Capitol, a grim and agonizing look is finally taken into Nazi Germany—into the new Nazi Germany of 1933, when Hitler took over the reins and a terrible wave of suppression and persecution

---

1. On October 3, 1940, after several months' effort, the German-American Bund dropped its suit against Warner Brothers. *The Confessions of a Nazi Spy* was one of the most popular films of 1939.

2. Most of the reviews included in Part Three from the *New York Times* by critic Bosley Crowther are fairly representative of general critical opinion of the propaganda films of the forties and fifties.

followed. And, on the basis of recorded facts and the knowledge that its drama is authentic, this picture turns out to be one of the most harrowing and inflammatory fictions ever placed upon the screen.

There is no use mincing words about it: *The Mortal Storm* falls definitely into the category of blistering anti-Nazi propaganda. It strikes out powerfully with both fists at the unmitigated brutality of a system which could turn a small and gemütlich university community into a hotbed of hatred and mortal vengeance, which could separate the loving members of a family and hound two free-thinking young people into flight from their homeland and to death. It gives no quarter to the antagonists; from clear-eyed and apparently upright young men, they suddenly become heartless sadists at nothing more than the call of their leader's name, the infectious chant of a song. There is no question of why they become such. The fact that they are is assumed as a premise.

But so violent is the oppression meted out by the Nazis and so bitter and hopeless is the fate of those against whom it is aimed that even the spiritual satisfaction which might be derived from a story of heroic suffering is seriously impaired, especially in the light of current headlines. As propaganda, *The Mortal Storm* is a trumpet call to resistance, but as theatrical entertainment it is grim and depressing today.

The story, as indicated, is a familiar and personal one. An eminent "non-Aryan" professor in a German university—presumably Munich—lives in comfort and honor amid his family and students until Hitler comes to power. Then, because he refuses to deny a scientific fact about human blood, he is sent to a concentration camp. His two stepsons become Nazis, his home is broken up. But his daughter and a former young man of the locality hold out against the rising tide. They are finally driven to flight, and, the house which was once filled with love and "gracious living" is left empty and desolate.

Although this tragic account has been pieced together out of a seven-year-old record of human suffering, the excellence of the production which Metro has given it—and the inherent forcefulness of a visual presentation—imbue *The Mortal Storm* with a sharp and seemingly contemporary reality. It is magnificently directed and acted. James Stewart and Margaret Sullavan bring to vibrant and anguished life the two young people who resist the sweeping system. Frank Morgan as the professor is superior as a gentle but resolute humanist. Robert Young plays the unsympathetic role of a Nazi zealot with convincing ostentation but limited penetration of the character. And fine performances also are given by Maria Ouspenskaya, Irene Rich, Bonita Granville, and many others.

The Mortal Storm is a passionate drama, struck out of the deepest tragedy, which is comforting at this time only in its exposition of heroic stoicism. As the oppressed professor says, "I've never prized safety, either for myself or my children. I've prized courage."

The Great Dictator

Bosley Crowther
(*The New York Times,* October 16, 1940)

The Great Dictator, based on an original story written, directed and produced by Charles Chaplin and released through United Artists; musical direction by Meredith Willson. At the Astor and Capitol Theatres.

People of the Palace

Adenoid Hynkel, Dictator of Tomania	Charles Chaplin
Benzini Napaloni, Dictator of Bacteria	Jack Oakie
Schultz	Reginald Gardiner
Garbitsch	Henry Daniell
Herring	Billy Gilbert
Mme. Napaloni	Grace Hayle
Bacterian Ambassador	Carter de Haven

People of the Ghetto

A Jewish Barber	Charles Chaplin
Hannah	Paulette Goddard
Mr. Jaeckel	Maurice Moscovich
Mrs. Jaeckel	Emma Dunn
Mr. Mann	Bernard Gorcey
Mr. Agar	Paul Weigel

Also Chester Conklin, Esther Michelson, Hank Mann, Florence Wright, Eddie Gribbon, Robert O. Davis, Eddie Dunn, Nita Pike and Peter Lynn.

Now that the waiting is over and the shivers of suspense at an end, let the trumpets be sounded and the banners flung against the sky. For the little tramp, Charlie Chaplin, finally emerged last night from behind the close-guarded curtains which have concealed his activities these past two years and presented himself in triumphal splendor as *The Great Dictator*—or you know who.

No event in the history of the screen has ever been anticipated with more hopeful excitement than the première of this film, which occurred simultaneously at the Astor and Capitol Theatres; no picture ever made has promised more momentous consequences. The prospect of little "Charlot," the most universally loved character in all the world, directing his superlative talent for ridicule against the most dangerously evil man alive has loomed as a titanic jest, a transcendent paradox. And the happy report this morning is that it comes off magnificently. *The Great Dictator* may not be the finest picture ever made—in fact, it possesses several disappointing shortcomings. But, despite them, it turns out to be a truly superb accomplishment by a truly great artist—and, from one point of view, perhaps the most significant film ever produced.

From the motion picture **The Great Dictator.** Courtesy of Museum of Modern Art.

Let this be understood, however: it is no catch-penny buffoonery, no droll and gentle-humored social satire in the manner of Chaplin's earlier films. *The Great Dictator* is essentially a tragic picture—or tragi-comic in the classic sense—and it has strongly bitter overtones. For it is a lacerating fable of the unhappy lot of decent folk in a totalitarian land, of all the hateful oppression which has crushed the humanity out of men's souls. And, especially, it is a withering revelation, through genuinely inspired mimicry, of the tragic weaknesses, the overblown conceit and even the blank insanity of a dictator. Hitler, of course.

The main story line is quite simple, though knotted with many complications. A little Jewish barber returns to his shop in the ghetto of an imaginary city (obviously Berlin) after a prolonged lapse of perception due to an injury in the World War. He does not know that the State is now under the sign of the double-cross, that storm troopers patrol the streets, that Jews are cruelly persecuted and that the all-powerful ruler of the land is one Hynkel, a megalo-maniac, to whom he bears—as a foreword states—a "coincidental resemblance." Thus, the little barber suffers a bitter disillusionment when he naively attempts to resist; he is beaten and eventually forced to flee to a neighboring country. But there he is mistaken for Hynkel, who has simultaneously annexed this neighboring land. And pushed upon a platform to make a conqueror's speech, he delivers instead a passionate appeal for human kindness and reason and brotherly love.

Thus, the story throws in pointed contrast the good man against the evil one—the genial, self-effacing but courageous little man of the street against the cold pretentious tyrant. Both are played by Chaplin, of course, in a highly comic vein, beneath which runs a note of eternal sadness. The little barber is our beloved Charlie of old—the fellow with the splay feet, baggy pants, trick mustache and battered bowler. And, as always, he is the pathetic butt of heartless circumstances, beaten, driven, but ever prepared to bounce back. In this role Chaplin performs two of the most superb bits of pantomine he has ever done—one during a sequence in which he and four other characters eat puddings containing coins to determine which shall sacrifice his life to kill the dictator, and the other a bit in which he shaves a man to the rhythm of Brahms's Hungarian Rhapsody.

But it is as the dictator that Chaplin displays his true genius. Whatever fate it was that decreed Adolf Hitler should look like Charlie must have ordained this opportunity, for the caricature of the former is devastating. The feeble, affected hand-salute, the inclination for striking ludicrous attitudes, the fabulous fits of rage and violent facial contortions—all the vulnerable spots of Hitler's exterior are pierced by Chaplin's pantomimic shafts. He is at his best in a wild senseless burst of guttural oratory—a compound of German, Yiddish and Katzenjammer double-talk; and he reaches positively exalted heights in a plaintive dance which he does with a large balloon representing the globe, bouncing it into the air, pirouetting beneath it—and then bursting into tears when the balloon finally pops.

Another splendid sequence is that in which Hynkel and Napaloni, a neighboring dictator, meet and bargain. Napaloni, played by Jack Oakie, is a bluff, expansive creature—the anthesis of neurotic Hynkel—and the two actors contrive in this part of the film one of the most hilarious lampoons ever performed on the screen. Others in the cast are excellent—Paulette Goddard as a little laundry girl, Henry Daniell as a Minister of Propaganda, Billy Gilbert as a Minister of War—but Oakie ranges right alongside Chaplin. And that is tops.

On the debit side, the picture is overlong, it is inclined to be repetitious and the speech with which it ended—the appeal for reason and kindness—is completely out of joint with that which has gone before. In it Chaplin steps out of character and addresses his heart to the audience. The effect is bewildering, and what should be the climax becomes flat and seemingly maudlin. But the sincerity with which Chaplin voices his appeal and the expression of tragedy which is clear in his face are strangely overpowering. Suddenly one perceives in bald relief the things which make *The Great Dictator* great—the courage and faith and surpassing love for mankind which are in the heart of Charlie Chaplin.

The Ramparts We Watch (1940)

[In 1940, Henry Luce's Time-Life Inc. organization released a feature-length episode of their March of Time series. The March of Time was a popular, journalistic short-subject series on contemporary news events which lasted throughout the 30s and 40s. Often, the reporting in these episodes was slanted toward the views of Time-Life Inc. (Moderately liberal, Republican, internationalist, etc.). The feature film (the only one of the series), *The Ramparts We Watch,* was a deliberate effort to propagandize for active American support of Britain and France against Germany. Using unknown actors, the film's setting is a small town in "middle America" from 1914 to 1918. At first, the people are provincial and isolationist, but after witnessing countless abuses, like unrestricted submarine warfare by Germany, their opinions gradually change and they become staunch supporters of American entry into World War I. The point of the film (which is made painfully obvious) is that the America of 1940 is in the same position as in 1917: She must take action against the new German aggressor.

Just prior to *Ramparts'* general release, Time-Life secured a print of the Nazi propaganda film, *Baptism of Fire* (mentioned in Part Two, p. 39). Editing it down to about 15 minutes, and substituting a German-accented, English narrator, the producers added it to *Ramparts* as a new ending.

The Ramparts We Watch received mixed reviews (as indicated in the following pages) and was not much of a box-office success. Hence, its value as propaganda is questionable. However, as you read over its promotional material, the pro and con reviews, and the newsclippings on the controversy it created, bear in mind that it represents one of the most overt propaganda films ever produced in America. It is doubly interesting considering its use of Nazi propaganda (*Baptism of Fire*) for reverse ends.]

By incorporating sections of the Nazi propaganda film, *Feuertaufe (Baptism of Fire)* as a new ending for *The Ramparts We Watch,* despite protests of the German Embassy, the March of Time has achieved a most dramatic effect for its first feature production, according to Producer Louis de Rochemont.

Beginning with a dramatic picturization of America in the First World War from the viewpoint of the citizens of a typical small town, the March of Time sought to draw the parallel with today's crisis when the world once more fears the consequences of a German victory. U.S. preparedness against such an eventuality was to be the keynote.

The Nazi film, designed to "soften" countries such as Norway, Holland, Belgium, and France, which Germany was about to conquer, was seen by the March of Time as a warning of what free countries were up against today. By

From film promotional material—R.K.O. Radio Pictures 1940, Lincoln Center Library of Performing Arts-Theater Collection—Microfilm reel 90, #541 (sections).

careful cutting, they believed it could be changed from Nazi terror propaganda to an inspiration to defeat these forces of aggression.

However, after weeks of negotiation with UFA, representing the German State Film Trust, for use of scenes from the film depicting the technique of the Polish Blitzkrieg, March of Time finally gave up the attempt when UFA imposed impossible demands for censorship, de Rochemont said.

Due to demands of exhibitors, *The Ramparts We Watch* was pre-released in a limited number of cities without the projected ending. Then, learning that the British Government had confiscated English language copies of *Baptism of Fire* through its alien property custodian at Bermuda, March of Time negotiated with John Grierson, Government Film Commissioner of Canada. The film was transferred by the Canadian Government to the March of Time which immediately set to work to incorporate the most significant sections of the film into *The Ramparts We Watch.*

In the Nazi sequences American moviegoers will now see for the first time a Stuka bomber diving in to destroy a railroad junction, the German war machine building bridges, razing Warsaw, spraying flaming gasoline on a trapped garrison. It will see parachute troops dropped behind the lines, panzer divisions in action, and fifth columnists pointing out those who "persecuted" them in order that they may be shot.

The new *Ramparts We Watch* won immediate critical acclaim when first shown to the public at the same time that Nazi officials were seeking to stop the showing of *Baptism of Fire* when shown as part of *The Ramparts We Watch.*

But such well known figures as H. V. Kaltenborn, famed radio commentator and student of propaganda methods, and Major George Fielding Eliot, outstanding U. S. military expert, agreed that "a way must be found to show *Baptism of Fire* to the American public."

As incorporated in *The Ramparts We Watch* according to Major Eliot, "it takes on a meaning the Germans did not foresee. Instead of terror, it inspires in the hearts of free men and women a hatred of Nazi methods and a grim resolution to defeat them."

The Ramparts We Watch

Bosley Crowther

(*The New York Times,* September 20, 1940)

The Ramparts We Watch, script by Robert L. Richards and Cedric R. Worth; produced and directed by Louis de Rochemont as the first full-length feature for The March of Time. At the Radio City Music Hall.

Dan Meredith .... John Adair
Joe Kovacs, Hungarian immigrant .... John Sommers

Mrs. Joe Kovacs	Julia Kent
Anna Kovacs	Ellen Prescott
Hon. John Lawton	C. W. Stowell
Mrs. John Lawton	Ethel Hudson
Edward Averill	Frank McCabe
Mrs. Averill	Myra Archibald
Walter Averill	Edward Wragge
Professor Gustav Bensinger	Alfredo U. Wyss
Mrs. Bensinger	Marguerite Brown
Hilda Bensinger	Georgette McKee
Fred Bensinger	Robert Rapelye
Stuart Gilchrist	Harry C. Stopher
Mrs. Gilchrist	Jane Stuart
Ralph Gilchrist	Elliott Reid
Mrs. Dora Smith	Augusta Durgeon
Eddie	Albert Gattiber
Tommy	Thomas S. Bernie Jr.
Capt. John Kellogg	H. G. Grady

Like the man who was suddenly switched from a diet of cream-puffs to hardtack, we find ourself this morning with a bite that is tough to chew. For the Music Hall, which has lately been feasting us all on frivolous fare, changed cooks on us yesterday and presented a meal of sobering roughage. It is listed on the cinematic menu by the name of *The Ramparts We Watch,* prepared as its first full-length feature by the staff of The March of Time. And a more provocative or challenging motion picture has not been placed before the public in years—or maybe, on second thought, never.

For the fact of the matter is that there has never been a motion picture just like this one. Started a year ago as a film account of the many devious forces which drew this country into the first World War, it underwent considerable revision to conform with shifts in the international scene during the last ten months. From a frankly exploratory document it changed gradually into a directive one. And now, with its showing at the Music Hall—after playing in various versions about the country—it emerges as a straight propaganda picture, solemnly bidding the people of this land to gird themselves for defense, bugling America to the alert.

Perhaps it is not the province of a critic to reveal such details about the making of a picture. But in this case it is pertinent, for the changes in the purport of the film were made to conform with a changing public attitude. And a nation which eight months ago felt comparatively secure and aloof from the echo of an old war abroad is today most alarmedly aware of a new and unpredictable menace. Wherefore *The Ramparts We Watch* is aimed to crystallize this shift in opinion by reminding our citizens of their former fight.

However, aside from its message, which is a matter for purely personal analysis, *The Ramparts We Watch* has much to excite the movie-goer. Produced along the same lines as the familiar March of Time shorts, it recounts through "pictorial journalism" the story of a great national crisis—the cumulations of a people's purpose. It is not an "entertainment" film, in the easy sense of that word, for it deals in historic facts as they fall into a grim, dramatic pattern. But it is an emotional film, and a stirring recreation of an era.

The story is that of America during the years 1914–18, as reflected in the lives of various people in a small American city. In 1914, it is a peaceful land, where people go to the picnic grove in open-air street cars, little boys ride on ice wagons and gay blades dance the Hesitation. Then war breaks out in Europe, America slowly begins to feel it. A foreign laborer leaves the small town for his homeland, people talk. Through old newsreel sequences, the course of world events is woven in with developments in the town. The Lusitania is sunk; America is outraged. Opinions clash; there are peace parades and advocates for preparedness. Wilson is re-elected. Training camps are started. There is sabotage in American munitions factories, armed neutrality, then war—all reflected in the emotions of the townsfolk.

The climactic sequence of the picture, which points the sickening parallel between events in those days and current happenings, is made up of clips from the Nazi picture, *Feuertaufe,*[1] a hideous account of the German invasion of Poland. This is said to be the picture which was shown in Norway and other nations to frighten the intended victims of Nazi aggression. It is the same picture which has been showing for several weeks at a small theatre up in Yorkville.[2]

By a brilliant conception of Louis de Rochemont, producer of the film, non-actors were used to play the numerous roles of the townsfolk, thus imparting the illusion of photographed actuality. Through this device, the old newsreel and the fictionized story blend perfectly.

One might reasonably contend that *The Ramparts We Watch* lacks suspense, that it drags in spots. One might hold that it tells a half-truth, that it should have pursued its first purpose. But no one can say that it does not recapture a memorable and poignant phase of our national life, that it fails to remind us effectively of our vital heritage.

---

1. *Baptism of Fire.*
2. The German section of New York City.

At Your Own Risk

Otis Fergusson

(*The New Republic*, August 5, 1940)

The March of Time is putting out a collection of old newsreels, stock shots and many bridging reënactments that runs the length of a feature picture and tells all in the title: *The Ramparts We Watch.* It is history and also rub-a-dub-dub. There are indications in the early sections that under the corporalship of Mr. Luce time was marching two ways at once, and that there might possibly be two sides to how fast we tossed young fellers into the overseas furnace; but by the end the purpose is pretty well straightened out.

Whatever the purpose, the effect of a thing like this lies in how well it is done. There have been several collections of World War shots that reached a higher emotional rise and climax—back in the days when raising boys to be soldiers was not being done in the better magazines, remember? But its over-all coverage of how the country felt and how the Wilson Cabinet and New York streets and ladies' hats and new Packards looked; what people were saying and singing and dancing to; what happened in church and in the schools and town meetings; who was being elected or run out of town—in this recreation of an era it is a handsome thing to see. In spite of the inevitable trace of stiltedness attaching to the people in documentaries who are set doing things as actors without really being actors, the little representative groups of students, gals, doctors, lawyers, politicians and journalists are put in motion with a nearer approach to things as they were than you find in memory. And the sound division has done a major job of recreation: you will hear every song of those days you can remember, and as many more you've forgotten. (But may I hope that some day some man who scores music will go listen to how a bugle call is played by a bugler, not a second-desk trumpet brought up on the Egmont Overture? It's a lot to ask, but a hope worth hoping, for a good bugler is one of the joys of life and may not be copied.)

Very well, the job is well done. And it touches on the mighty theme of a nation coming to life and to arms. It is stirring. Very well, stirring to what?

Here is where the objections come in, and the question: even granting it is all truth, which it isn't, how much of the whole truth is it? Was the war as easy as that? A few ships, a few shell-bursts, many men marching and some of them rather dirty? A German or two eased off a homeguard committee? Liberty Loans for liberty and not to buy up the bag Morgan and Company was holding? Khaki and shoes and guns turned out with a busy will for the boys over there and none of them paper, or backfiring? No disillusion but a few brave tears of a mother? American boys in France saying "Vive la France" and Frenchmen in cabarets saying "Vive Vilson" and nothing, absolutely nothing else to the AEF? Barracks and no slackers, no objectors? No beatings and witch hunts? Really?

The fever, the national will, the whoop and hoorah were all true at the time, no doubt. So was the world square once; so were the lives of men dependent on the will of the little people. Now we know otherwise—or we did yesterday. And to leave out what we have learned, to say for truth what we know was false, to pass over the misery, the stupidity, the greed, the waste and slaughter, is to blow up a great recruiting poster, an invitation to leave your head outside. We may be proud to be America. We may be ready to stand back of it. But these are just the times when we should turn away from any group of cheapjacks using such times and such high and noble emotions for nothing in the world but to sell their stinking little tent show. I'm afraid this film comes with very good timing, and I know it is done as smooth as oil. But we should have learned by now. If that's what you want, America, take it away.

Time Marches Back

Margaret Frakes
(*The Christian Century,* October 16, 1940)

"Historians who write *now* about what happened *then* can never show the past as past. They write . . . with the falsifying aid of hindsight." This is the warning which Archibald MacLeish, librarian of Congress and Pulitzer prize winner, addresses to the American people in a two-page advertisement in a recent issue of *Life,* his purpose being to promote the March of Time's feature-length movie, *The Ramparts We Watch.*

The gentlemen of the March of Time, it seems, are concerned about what you and I think about the First World War. They know that for years we have been subjected to what they see as the "propaganda" of the historians. We have been, as Mr. MacLeish says, "looking at the First World War in the perspective of the historian's hindsight." Doing so, we have discovered a number of what they consider to be untruths. We have come to believe, for instance, that perhaps something other than the rapaciousness of a people led by a cruel old man bent on world domination was the cause of that war. We have been led to suspect that some of the atrocity stories were, to put it mildly, exaggerated. We have found traces of British propaganda. We have even begun to bring to light signs of something that looks strangely like self-interest on the part of American bankers and manufacturers and producers of raw materials.

So the March of Time has set out to correct that hindsight, to take us back to the days of the First World War, to show us how it *really* was.

The Ramparts We Watch shows an American community from 1914 through the war years. Everyday people in New London, Connecticut, act the story of what the editors choose to tell us happened in those years. At first, the war is far away. But gradually—much too gradually, the film hints—the people begin to wake up. The ruthless Germans violate Belgium. Boys go across to help France and Britain stem the forces of evil and some of them are killed. Unrestrained submarine warfare begins. The Lusitania is sunk. People begin to get excited. The film lets us, indeed, hear one pacifist song—but it is sung in a restaurant haunted by beer-drinking German-Americans. All this time, the government and business are strangely apathetic. Then our ships are told where they can and cannot go. Now we really get angry. Imagine telling an American what he can do! So we—the common people—force the issue, and our leaders are compelled to let us have our way. We go out to fight for our rights and for democracy. (Not as quickly, of course, as we should have, since we were, then as now, blind and trusting and therefore unprepared, and so it took us too long to get going.) But anyway, we finally arrive in France. And we save freedom for the world.

But we weren't courageous enough. We let historians falsify what we had done and find other motives for events. Now, our precious liberty is threatened again. And the March of Time, fearful lest now we permit our thinking to be colored by what we have learned in these twenty years about the motives and the currents behind that war, takes us back and lets us feel the emotions of those years—deliberately ignoring what has been learned since, cheerfully indicating that now is the time to act in just the same manner again, to go out in moral indignation to fight against a similar evil rampant again in the world.

As Pare Lorentz, himself a maker of documentary films and movie critic for *McCalls,* points out, *The Ramparts We Watch* errs for the most part in omission. There is nothing, he notes, of the "extraordinary propaganda campaign" which preceded our declaration of war, of the bumper cotton crop of 1914 which had so much to do with the determination to protect our exports, of Colonel House, of the senior La Follette. There is no mention, in the concluding sections which deal with the rise of the present crisis, of the Chamberlain government, of the war in Spain, of the things our foreign correspondents have been telling us for years, of the currents at work behind the European scene. We are to be induced to believe simply that, as he interprets it, we "were patient and forbearing until the Germans became so arrogant we couldn't stand it any longer" and that now we "are faced with a necessity of preparing to go to war again." The result of such omission, it follows, is that truth takes a holiday.

The closing sequences of this film now consist of the German movie, *The Baptism of Fire,* which shows how total warfare is practiced by the German army, particularly as it entered Poland. This is obvious propaganda, designed to convince prospective enemies of the might of the German forces. Inserted in *The Ramparts We Watch* with appropriate comments written by the American producers it serves the purpose which they have in mind, which is to convince the American people that the German menace threatens today even more than in 1917, and that our only recourse is to plunge into a gigantic armament program to get ready for battle with our future foes.

Incidentally, the March of Time's method of acquiring the German film raises a fine point. The editors had sought to acquire title from UFA, the German distributing company, which had refused unless the sound track accompanying the film should be left intact. Finally, however, a print of the film was seized as contraband by British authorities in Bermuda as it came in by clipper plane. It was seized in order to keep it from reaching the American public as German propaganda. But as soon as the British authorities were assured that Mr. Luce's bright young men would so doctor up the sound track as to make it good British propaganda, it was turned over to the March of Time, which proceeded to fit in a new sound track, with thinly veiled taunts and insults by a German-accented commentator. As the film is shown, there is nothing to indicate that this commentary has been substituted for the original, nor to indicate that it is being presented to American audiences by arrangement with the British censor.

All this, we are led to understand, is for "the defense of this democracy." One wonders, however, while watching the monthly March of Time shorts on the screen, whether it is for defense alone that the editors of this most widely promoted newsreeel are waging preparedness. *Gateways to Panama,* the most recent release, plays up danger spots in South America such as the French penal colony in Guiana. In addition to pointing out the defense value of the newly acquired air and navy bases in the Caribbean, it manages to suggest that our policing powers over the northern coast of South America could be much increased.

Spoils of Conquest, the preceding release, features the Dutch East Indies, emphasizing the importance to the axis powers—and to us in case of war—of their vast wealth. It shows the Dutch colonists making almost a heaven on earth for the natives. (There is no comment on it, but almost every shot of an industrial scene shows native *children* at work.) Then Japan is shown eyeing the wealth of the islands, and the commentator's tone grows meanacing. It trembles as the home-loving Dutch are pictured preparing their puny defenses, and it rings out a challenge as a fleet is shown, the fleet to which these people look with anxious, hopeful eyes—the United States fleet at anchor in the Philippines. Charts outside theaters showing this release explain how that fleet could checkmate Japan's moves in eastern waters. Considerably more than propaganda for defense alone, this would seem.

The release on the Philippines shows the islands coming to regret the approaching withdrawal of American protection, fearful lest Japan seize their wealth—a thing which, the film suggests, we should never allow to come to pass. One wonders even more whether it is actually defense in which this newsreel is interested when one views the release on the United States navy, which ends with views of the marines, fully equipped, embarking to be "trained to fight," the commentator tells us in ringing tones, "as they have always been trained to fight, *offensive war.*"

There will be other releases in the preparedness series, no doubt. One can safely predict from these which have already been released the course they will take. The March of Time, being partly staged and acted out for the camera and accompanied by a commentary like the voice of doom itself, is more dangerous than the regular newsreels, which so far have been for the most part straight-forward presentations of events. Of course, the other reels show a super-abundance of war material. But in the current state of the world, this is to be expected. Recently a Chicagoan, just returned from a visit to Mexico, expressed in a local newspaper his surprise and regret on dropping into a Mexican theater to discover an American newsreel devoted entirely to the production of arma-ments in the United States. At the least, he felt, Mexicans would get the idea that we were "a very warlike nation." Perhaps we are.

Variety, trade paper of the amusement world, reported early in June that army chiefs had met with motion picture executives to determine what part the cinema industry should play in boosting the nation's defense program. Producers were inclined to fear public reaction to outright propaganda in feature films, no matter how cleverly concealed (an indication, by the way, of the producers' growing respect for audience discrimination). Defense preparation should be shown, they felt, only in newsreels and other shorts devoted to actual events. A recent *New York Times* story, however, reports another conclave of exhibitors as giving assurance that the nation's screens would be available at any time for whatever use the government deemed necessary for the defense program. A *Variety* story tells of the production by the Warner studio of a series of shorts in technicolor to promote army service. The same studio is planning, too, some full-length films dealing with preparedness.

So far there has been little actual propaganda for preparedness in feature films. A pacifist in *Foreign Correspondent* turns out to be a nazi spy, and characters in all sorts of pictures have suddenly developed a surprising habit of holding forth on the benefits of Americanism. But this, again, is to be expected. *The Mortal Storm, Four Sons, The Man I Married, Pastor Hall*—all anti-nazi films—picture the horrors of a regimented state, but it is always easier to point out the tragic drama in the sins of others than to look honestly at our own shortcomings. Moreover, no one can fairly claim that these films make any direct effort to hustle this country along the road to war.

Presentation of the dangers to our democracy, of the sickening reality of "total war"—by all means let us have it, and vividly. But the March of Time releases are crying in almost evangelistic tones: "Turn back! Forget what we have learned since the First World War. Feel, believe just as we did then. America must be first!" And it is the falsifying emotion of those years—as of today—rather than any "falsifying" hindsight that will be our destruction. These releases are not so much anti-fascist as a presentation of a sort of *America über alles,* a picture of Americans as a people destined to protect the wealth of the Indies and the future of the entire Western hemisphere. As such, would we not become what we seek to overcome?

Pennsylvania Ban
on "Ramparts" Film

(*The New York Times,* September 19, 1940)

Harrisburg, Pa., Sept. 18 (AP)—A Harrisburg theatre closed today after running for matinee audiences the picture *The Ramparts We Watch,* containing a reel barred by the Pennsylvania Board of Censors as "part of the fear propaganda being disseminated by Germany."

Robert H. Sidman, the theatre manager who had announced defiance of the censors' order, said he acted on advice of counsel that further showing would be "illegal," unless the last reel were deleted.

An agreement was reached, he said, with the producers of the picture, and the Pennsylvania Attorney General's office for a reshowing at the Philadelphia office of the Board of Censors tomorrow.

Mrs. Edna Carroll of Philadelphia, chairman of the board, said the producers substituted the "objectionable" reel before the picture was to receive a trial showing in Harrisburg and Reading today. The picture in its original form was approved by the board on Aug. 9.

Reading Theatre Goes Ahead

Reading, Pa., Sept. 18—Ignoring threats by the State Board of Motion Picture Censors to close his theatre and confiscate the *Ramparts We Watch* film, put on the screen at its Pennsylvania première here today, Cornelius G. Keeney, manager of the Park Theatre, went ahead with the presentation of the picture.

Notified that the final reel of the *Baptism of Fire* part of the picture, screened in Germany, had been banned by the State board, Mr. Keeney instructed his attorney, George Eves, to obtain a Berks court injunction against closing his theatre and confiscation of the picture by the State police.

After a parade of National Guardsmen to publicize the film Mr. Keeney was host to the guardsmen at tonight's showing.

One of the Park's lessees is Jay Emanuel, Philadelphia picture magazine publisher.

First notice of disapproval of the last reel was received by Mr. Keeney from Dr. Francis B. Haas, State Superintendent of Public Instruction, who said the State police will close the house and confiscate the film, if shown.

Identical Version Passed Here

The prints of *The Ramparts We Watch,* which have been banned in Pennsylvania, are identical with the version which will open locally this morning at the Radio City Music Hall, it was said last night at the offices of The March of Time. This version, including the disputed *Baptism of Fire* sequences, has been passed by the New York Board of Censors, it was said.

Louis de Rochemont, producer of The March of Time, who was reached by telephone in Philadelphia last night, stated that the picture would be resubmitted to the censors this morning and that an attempt would be made to obtain a reversal.

According to Mr. de Rochemont the disputed sequences were obtained from the Canadian Government after they had been confiscated by British contraband control officers at Bermuda. The picture which, it was said, was being sent here for propaganda purposes, is reported to be the same as that which German officials showed to the officials of Norway and to representatives of the Low countries before those territories were invaded.

Ramparts Ban Upheld

Philadelphia, Oct. 1—Three judges of Common Pleas Court No. 3 today upheld the ban imposed by the State Board of Censors on the motion picture, *The Ramparts We Watch.* They held that the censors had not abused their discretion, as contended by the producers.

The opinion, by Judges Howard A. Davis, Byron A. Milner and Raymond MacNeille, said that the German-made film *Baptism of Fire,* which was added to the original version, portrayed "actual scenes of the German conquest of Poland, with accompanying language manifestly intended by the Nazi regime in Germany as propaganda designed to disseminate Nazi doctrines, and to induce other peoples into submitting to German domination, or to the adoption of the Nazi ideology."

The appellants, RKO Pictures, Inc., and Time, Inc., will appeal the decision to the Pennsylvania Supreme Court.[1]

---

1. The Pennsylvania Supreme Court upheld the Philadelphia ban on the film on October 2, 1940.

WORLD WAR II
Hollywood at War

When the United States entered World War II, isolationism was no longer a sentiment to contend with (Pearl Harbor took care of that). Now the Hollywood movie reflected American patriotism. Despite initial setbacks to U. S. troops in the Pacific in the early days of the War, the film industry produced a series of grim, yet heroically optimistic combat pictures showing American defeats at places like Wake Island and Bataan in the spirit of the Alamo. The American fighting man was portrayed as a tough, rugged individualist, shaking his empty gun or fist at the evil enemy and spouting heroic phrases like "Tell 'em to come and get us," or "Surrender, hell!" Several of these combat films deliberately sought to unify the American war spirit by creating "all-American" regiments. Hence in *Bataan* (cited in this section and typical of this genre of film) the fighting force includes a Jew, a Pole, a Black, a Chicano, a pacifist, a teenager, an army "regular," and even a criminal. However melodramatic such films are, they represent a reasonably skillful, reinforcing type of propaganda. Americans, by and large, were vehemently behind the World War II effort, and heroic, "integrated" combat films like those cited in this section provided some vicarious military identification for audiences. Another factor about such films was their portrayal of the enemy. The pompous "Krauts" and sneaky "Japs" were even more stereotyped than the American soldiers. According to Hollywood, these "types" were the enemy that had to be wiped out.

Although such oversimplified portrayals now seem a throwback to the old World War I epics, many of these films met with critical acclaim and box-office popularity. Indeed when a film finally was made which portrayed an enemy as more brilliant and cunning than the Americans in it, the dean of film critics, Bosley Crowther, virtually accused its makers of being unpatriotic. That film, *Lifeboat* (1944), was also an anti-German propaganda film, but from a completely different point of view, as you will see by reading a section of its screenplay and the debate over its effects between Mr. Crowther and Kenneth Macgowan, its producer.

Wake Island

Bosley Crowther

(*The New York Times,* September 2, 1942)

Wake Island, screen play by W. R. Burnett and Frank Butler, from the records of the United States Marine Corps; directed by John Farrow for Paramount. At the Rivoli.

Major Caton	Brian Donlevy
Joe Doyle	Robert Preston
Lieut. Bruce Cameron	Macdonald Carey
Shad McCloskey	Albert Dekker
Aloysius (Smacksie) Randall	William Bendix
Commander Reynolds	Walter Abel
Ivan Probenski	Mikhail Rasumny
Sergeant Higbee	Bill Goodwin
Sally Cameron	Barbara Britton
Captain Patrick	Damian O'Flynn

Now that the United States Marine Corps has given the Japs a dose of medicine in the Solomons and is poising, from all accounts, for further thrusts, this is a time for grim reflection upon a score which the Leathernecks have to pay off. Such a stern medication—and a rousing tribute, too—is Paramount's new film, *Wake Island,* which came to the Rivoli last night. Here, in all its harsh and bitter detail, in all its deathless gallantry, is the story of the small Marine garrison which held that tiny Pacific isle for the two terrible weeks after Pearl Harbor and went down fighting, brave and defiant to the end.

Here is a film which should surely bring a surge of pride to every patriot's breast. And here is a film for which its makers deserve a sincere salute. Except for the use of fictional names and a very slight contrivance of plot, it might be a literal document of the manner in which the Wake detachment of Marines fought and died in the finest tradition of their tough and indomitable corps. For Paramount has tactfully resisted all the obvious temptations to beat the drum. It has made a realistic picture about heroes who do not pose as such—about a group of hard-bitten soldiers who lie in their fox-holes and man their observation posts with never a big theatrical gesture or a comment that doesn't ring true. And when, after two weeks of pounding, their weary major answers a challenge to give up with the simple words, "Tell 'em to come and get us," the epitome of soldier terseness is marked.

Obviously, the story of Wake Island needed no dramatic dressing up. Drama more taut than any fiction was played on that desolate moon of sand. And so, W. R. Burnett and Frank Butler, in their script simply outlined characters—a square-jawed, quiet-spoken Marine major, a civilian builder who blusters a bit, a couple of Devildog rowdies, a taciturn flyer and other honest types—and put them up against the situation which history too plainly records. There is no necessity for inspiring any juvenile delinquents with zeal; no unsuspected hero suddenly rockets to undying fame. Each man does his duty in his own efficient way. Each man dies as men die, by crumbling in a heap. The stubborn defense of Wake Island was—and is—a full-sized drama by itself.

Credit Director John Farrow with giving the film much brutal suspense, for drawing the story taut with screaming action and intervals of breathless quiet. The tangible solidity of his setting—a location on the Salton Sea in California—impinges the film with a reality which is heightened by the visible evidence of exploding bombs. No one who sees *Wake Island* can complain that he doesn't know what a bombardment is.

In the role of the Marine major, Brian Donlevy is a credit to the corps, not to mention the acting profession. And Albert Dekker and Macdonald Carey are likewise apt. But William Bendix and Robert Preston will snag the plaudits for their performances as tough Marines. A more respectable pair of Leathernecks has not come along since Flagg and Quirt. Particularly Mr. Bendix. He's a partner for any fox-hole. His withering rejoinder to Mr. Preston's observation that the Japs are blowing them to bits is of truly legendary magnificence—"Whatd'ya care? It ain't your island, is it?"

This reviewer first saw *Wake Island* at the Quantico Marine base last week. On that occasion, some 2,000 fighters cheered it with thunderous applause. Those Marines have a personal interest involved. We will confidently stand on their response.

Bataan

Bosley Crowther
(*The New York Times*, June 4, 1943)

Bataan: original screen play by Robert D. Andrews; directed by Tay Garnett; produced by Irving Starr for Metro-Goldwyn-Mayer. At the Capitol.

Sergeant Bill Dane	Robert Taylor
Lieut. Steve Bentley	George Murphy
Corp. Jake Feingold	Thomas Mitchell
Corp. Barney Todd	Lloyd Nolan
Capt. Henry Lassiter	Lee Bowman
Leonard Purckett	Robert Walker

Felix Ramirez .... Desi Arnaz
F. X. Matowski .... Barry Nelson
Matthew Hardy .... Phillip Terry
Corp. Juan Katigbak .... Roque Espiritu
Wesley Eeps .... Kenneth Spencer
Yankee Salazar .... J. Alex Havier
Sam Malloy .... Tom Dugan

Perhaps the world will never know the whole story of the heroic defense of Bataan—of sick men who died fighting in fox-holes with not a survivor to tell how they died, of brave deeds and noble sacrifices performed where no friendly eye could see. Perhaps the full record of that ordeal is already lost in the silences of time. But, for all the limitations of a studio and the general tendency of Hollywood to cheat a bit, a surprisingly credible conception of what that terrible experience must have been for some of the men who endured it—the grim attrition of body and mind—is inexorably presented by Metro in a harrowing picture tersely titled *Bataan*.

This time, at least, a studio hasn't purposely "prettified" facts. This time it has made a picture about war in true and ugly detail. There is nothing bright or exultant about this new film at the Capitol—nothing except the admiration inspired by the image of brave men hanging on. There is sickening filth and bloodshed in it. Men die with marrow-chilling screams. Death is a grim inevitability. There are no optimists in the fox-holes of *Bataan*.

For this is a typical story of those last days on that scarred peninsula—the story of thirteen battered fighters grouped together to hold a rear point while the American and Filipino armies fell back on Corregidor. There is a young and nervous captain (Lee Bowman), who is picked off early by snipers. There is a hard-bitten sergeant (Robert Taylor), who inherits the improvised command when an Air Force lieutenant (George Murphy) relinquishes it to him on practical grounds. And there are nine grimy soldiers and one kid sailor—widely assorted as to type—who are tacitly labeled "expendable" for the purpose of holding a ravine.

And that's all there is to the story—just a nerve-racking, long-drawn account of how this nondescript rear-guard wreck a stone bridge and then stand by to keep the Japanese from building it back, while one after another the men are picked off until only the sergeant remains. And he, at the end, dies fighting from the edge of his own self-dug grave.

It is an obviously fabricated story as Robert D. Andrews has written it, mechanically packed with incidents, some of them moving and some of them not. It depends very largely on the nature and familiarity of the situations. The prayer of a Spanish-born soldier as he dies of malaria is maudlin. The prayer of a Negro soldier over the jungle grave of the dead captain is eloquent. There is too much determined heroism in the sacrificial gesture of the Air Force lieutenant when, mortally wounded, he orders his plane loaded with dynamite so he can dive it onto the critical bridge. And there is throat-choking, hot, close reality in the scenes of hand-to-hand combat with the Japanese. Tay Garnett's direction has emphasized tension much more respectably than it has framed attitudes.

The performances are consequently spotty. Robert Walker, a newcomer, is fine as the sailor, a garrulous youngster, as green and pliant as a sapling branch, whose emotions rush unguardedly to the surface and send wistful signals to your heart. Kenneth Spencer has quiet strength and simple dignity as a Negro soldier from the engineers—a character whose placement in the picture is one of the outstanding merits of it. And Mr. Taylor is believable as the sergeant, even though he does rush about a bit too much with a dark scowl. Lloyd Nolan is inclined, at moments, to overdo the "wise-guy" side of a renegade, though he comes through nicely at the climax, while Mr. Murphy is good until that last scene in the plane. Tom Dugan, Desi Arnaz and Alex Havier are convincing in soldier roles, and Thomas Mitchell plays his usual Irish iron-man, even though he is called Corporal Jake Feingold.

There are melodramatic flaws in *Bataan* and it contains some admitted technical mistakes. But it still gives a shocking conception of the defense of that bloody point of land. And it doesn't insult the honor of dead soldiers, which is something to say for a Hollywood film these days.

Bataan, a Promotion Release

[M.G.M.'s *prepared review* (standard for promotions of the time) is a good sample of the kind of national unity spirit early World War II films hoped to stir up.]

BATAAN VIVID FILM SHOWING LAST DITCH FIGHT OF 13 HEROES

The last stand fight of thirteen "expendable" men during the evacuation of the retreating but undefeated American Army in Bataan forms the theme of a gripping drama in *Bataan*, a remarkably vivid story of heroism under fire and now showing at the . . . theatre.

Thirteen men are detailed to blow up a bridge and hold the area, covering General MacArthur. Machine guns are set in fox-holes and Japanese snipers pick off victims. Sergeant Bill Dane (Robert Taylor) believes Corp. Barney Todd (Lloyd Nolan) to be a man who is wanted for murder.

The men blow up the bridge, settle in their shelters, and grimly hold off the enemy. Malaria attacks some of them. They are under constant fire. One by one the heroes are killed, until Taylor, firing his machine gun from his own grave, is the last remaining defender.

The picture gives Taylor the most realistic role of his career as the grim, heroic sergeant. The other featured players depict a cross-section of American life. George Murphy plays a young pilot. Thomas Mitchell is Corp. Jake Feingold. Roque Espiritu plays a Filipino volunteer; Desi Arnaz is a jitterbug from California; Kenneth Spencer a Negro soldier with a song for each burial.

Tay Garnett directed with skill and utmost realism. The locale is a fever-infested jungle. Others in the cast are Lee Bowman, Robert Walker, Barry Nelson, Phillip Terry, Tom Dugan, Alex Havier and Donald Curtis.

Spectacular battle sequences, the dynamiting of a bridge, thrilling clashes of Americans and Japanese cram the picture with action, while the drama is worked out in the human relationships under fire.

Adrift in "Lifeboat"

Bosley Crowther
(*The New York Times,* January 23, 1944)

[The next piece is Bosley Crowther's response to a letter written to *The New York Times* by Kenneth Macgowan, producer of *Lifeboat* in response to Mr. Crowther's original review of the film. The Macgowan letter follows the Crowther response to it. Following that is part of the dialogue from *Lifeboat.*]

Unless we had seen it with our own eyes, we would never in this world have believed that a film could have been made in this country in the year 1943 which sold out the democratic ideal and elevated the Nazi "superman." Certainly we would never have imagined that such a picture could have been made by the estimable director, Alfred Hitchcock, from a story by John Steinbeck. Yet such is the picture *Lifeboat,* which drifted into the Astor the other day. And this writer sits here in consternation at the appalling folly which it represents.

What in the name of heaven has happened to the judgment of men in Hollywood to permit such a blundering misconstruction—for misconstruction it certainly must have been! Where were the wits of Mr. Hitchcock and Mr. Steinbeck—not to mention everyone else who had a hand in this picture—that they did not immediately perceive the alarming implications of their carefully developed dramatic plot? Kenneth Macgowan, the producer, tells us in a letter printed below that the film was originally projected as a sort of one-set stunt and that a theme emerged suddenly and surprisingly after the characters and plot had been laid out. Didn't anyone then see the curious anti-democratic angle of that theme—or think of its effect upon the audience? What's going on out there?

For the benefit of those who are just now hearing of this shocking political aspect of *Lifeboat,* let us give you a careful analysis of its admittedly symbolic contents. It opens with a shot of the funnel of a torpedoed freighter sinking beneath the waves, and then, after sweeping the littered waters, it picks up a drifting lifeboat. Seated within this dismal vessel is a surprisingly sleek and elegant dame, wearing a beautiful mink coat and taking pictures with a movie camera. But soon the boat fills up with survivors, until there are nine of them in all—eight from the torpedoed freighter and one from the Nazi sub that did for her. (It seems that the sub was picked off by a final shot from the stricken ship.)

Now these eight survivors from the freighter represent quite obviously a studiously selected cross-section of the peoples of the democratic world. There is the richly turned out lady, representative of the luxury fringe—a callous and cynical worldling, rather colorful but strictly for herself. Then there is a brisk and somewhat pompous American business tycoon who is also cynical, patronizing and playing his own single hand. Next there are two wistful women, one an emotionally frustrated Army nurse and the other an English housewife who has lost her baby and very soon goes over the side. Finally there are four assorted crewmen who represent, apparently, the working class—an oiler, a deckhand, a radio operator and a humble Negro steward.

All right, here's a passable selection of democratic folks to set against the German for the principal conflict of the film. But what do Mr. Hitchcock and Mr. Steinbeck do right away? They set these eight survivors to wrangling among themselves. First question is which one of them is going to command the boat, and immediately it is apparent that no one is fit to command. The business tycoon assumes authority but is straightaway howled down. The radio operator is suggested, but he admits his inadequacy. Then the burly oiler, who is the toughest one of the eight, announces himself as commander and virtually gets it by default. Mr. Macgowan has objected to our remark in our review of the film that the group "did not choose their own leader." He says that they did. But if this represented election, we still think it hopelessly weak.

Anyhow, the point is that no one of the democratic folks possesses resource or ability or the confidence of all the rest. And soon it is apparent that the German is the only man in the boat who has the coolness and the know-how to take over leadership. He amputates the leg of the deckhand when nobody else can do so, and he grabs the tiller and gives orders when the others are floundering around in a storm. True, it develops that the German was the captain of the sub, which naturally explains his qualifications and his superiority in this spot. But hold—that's how the dramatists ordained it. And, don't forget, this is a symbolic film.

Mr. Macgowan—and, presumably, Mr. Hitchcock—seem to feel that vindication is achieved for their democratic peoples when they kill the Nazi captain out of rage. He has just dumped the crippled deckhand, dying of thirst and delirious, into the sea while the others slept because the deckhand has discovered that he has a secret water-flask. The German also has in his possession, as he confesses, some vitamin pills, which he uses to keep his strength up so he can row the boat to a Nazi supply ship. Furious, then, at the German for drowning the weakened deckhand, the rest of the survivors jump on him and hysterically beat him to death. Mark you, they didn't kill him when they first discovered that he was rowing them to the ship; they accepted that sad eventuality in a miserable, defeatist way. They only take violent measures when their blood-for-blood lust is aroused.

Is this vindication for pusillanimity and ineffectualness up to this point? Is this a respectable symbolization of the rise of the democracies? If it is, we fail to perceive it. For the killing is done in ugly rage, and after it is accomplished the people are still without resolve. "Maybe," mutters the tycoon, "one of us ought to try to row. But where to? What for? When we killed the German, we killed our motor." That doesn't sound like resolute talk to us! Nor is the Negro's response very practical. "We've still got a motor," he says. "Who?" asks the literal-minded tycoon. The Negro looks mutely toward the sky.

At that, the Negro is clairvoyant, for certainly these people do not save themselves. They make a clumsy effort to catch fish with diamonds for bait, but abandon the fish and beg for capture when the Nazi ship appears. And it is only through divine intervention from a warship on the horizon that they, representing the democracies, are pulled out of the soup. What is that warship, symbolically, to the little world contained in this boat? A miracle obviously—a guardian angel. Is that all we have to depend upon? Apparently the dramatists thought so, for the democrats are still unresolved, still vacillating before the dilemma of a second German picked up from the sea, when the fade-out is ultimately reached.

No matter how much Mr. Macgowan endeavors to subordinate the theme to the purely stunt aspects of this picture the theme is the most significant thing. And it is the thing which makes it most dangerous, especially because the film is so cleverly constructed, so well acted and so dramatically intriguing all the way that audiences follow it intently in wonder and anxiety. Yet its final, insidious implication is that the democratic peoples are weak—not only weak but vacillating—and that the Nazi is resourceful and resolved.

This is precisely the reason why we view the whole thing with alarm. Any form of propaganda which invades the mind with a doubt is harmful. Is this the conception of ourselves that we want to show abroad? Is this a picture of civilians which we want our soldiers on the fronts to see? Is this, in short, an honest symbolization of our democratic strength? In the reasoned opinion of this writer it definitely is not.

The Producer Explains

To the Screen Editor:

Yes, *Lifeboat* does have a theme. As that fifth wheel of film making—the producer—I must tell you how delighted I was to find the theme coming to the surface through the progressing paragraphs of your critic's review. He saw that these images of the democracies huddled together in the boat were facing a superman out of the Herrenvolk, and must ultimately rise up to kill him. But at the end I was a bit dismayed and chagrined to discover that he hadn't seen the theme as completely as Hitchcock, Steinbeck, Swerling and I had intended. He felt that we had made a poor case for the democracies and too good a one for the representative of Germany.

The review says that the German assumed command of the boat "when the others cannot choose their own leader." This is not quite accurate. They do choose their own leader and they try to keep the German in his place of isolation. It is the storm that alters this. In the emergency the German, with a scheme in mind, seizes control. Also, our people do not accept the "prospect of a concentration camp as better than death" merely because of their own free will. They are starving and athirst. The German has water and condensed food and energy tablets. Even so, when the German's iniquities come clear in his murder of Gus, the men and women summon the desperate strength to end his rule. He has been as resourceful as the Nazis; as courageous, as unscrupulous and as damnably vicious. Against him our people have been uncertain, weak, footling, but finally victorious.

If we have muffed our theme I am truly sorry. But may I explain the rather interesting fact that the theme was an accident—an inevitable one perhaps—in the making of what we hoped to be an exciting and truthful film.

Lifeboat began simply as Hitchcock's suggestion that we should lay an entire picture in a lifeboat and thus turn out the first one-set feature film ever made. Next, he contributed the basic dramatic skeleton—the German U-boat captain thrust among his victims and plotting against them. Steinbeck then wrote a story which provided most of the characters and certain of the events. At this point Jo Swerling stepped in and began the working out of the actual plot and script in collaboration with the director.

Up to that point—indeed, far beyond it—we had not the slightest notion of building a theme. We built it, however, quite unconsciously, and suddenly awoke to that fact. Unwittingly we had set images of the "soft democracies" into a little world dominated in will and purpose by an aggressor. We found them steering themselves past a sort of Munich only to run smack against a Warsaw. We saw a common rising of civilized people pressed too far.

Your critic saw this—as we did—but he followed us no further. Because we allowed our people to be rescued by the only thing that ever rescues people at sea—the sheer accident of a ship on the horizon—he felt we were letting down our theme and leaving the German still superman and our people craven. I don't think so, for our people rose to one more final effort in the attempt to catch fish, and we certainly polished off the German as just as thorough a scoundrel and just as "ersatz" a superman as his own Hitler.

I'm truly sorry that your critic didn't note the other bit of theme that we tried to provide—this time consciously—which was the injection of a second German into the boat. When we recognized that, unwittingly, we had built a symbol of our war, Hitchcock asked how we were to end the picture along this thematic line. We had shown the German go down in defeat and our little party come through into peace—the peace of rescue. Figuratively the war was over. What, asked Hitchcock, are we going to do with Germany after the war? He suggested that the boat pick up a young German sailor from the sunken supply ship. We did pick him up. We saw the varied reactions of the people of the boat. "He's just a boy." "He's wounded." "Don't trust him." "No, nurse him." "Hell! (or the Hays equivalent). Throw him back into the sea!" At which point the Nazi pulls a gun, is disarmed, and held for future reckoning.

If we have failed in making our theme completely clear, at least we may defend ourselves by saying that we didn't set out to make a symbolic film and we never let the possibilities of the theme divert us from our first object—the shaping of a film with as much excitement and reality as we could summon under challenging technical limitations.

Kenneth Macgowan
Los Angeles, Calif.
Jan. 14, 1944.

Lifeboat, Script Excerpts

Dialogue only—taken from the screen (no directions) Dec. 31, 1943. Copyright 20th Century-Fox Film Corp. Screenplay by Jo Swerling; story by John Steinbeck.

[Willi, the Nazi U-boat captain (Walter Slezak), has demoralized the crew of the tiny vessel by demonstrating able seamanship (he's got a hidden compass, which the audience can see, but the crew cannot), and boundless energy (he's secretly taking water and energy pills). He has just thrown the wounded, feverish, and delirious Gus (William Bendix) overboard. Now the crew begins to realize Willi's secrets (he's convinced them to row to Germany until this point). The members of the crew confront Willi about Gus's death. Note the differences between the pro-Allied sentiments in the following sequences compared to those of *Bataan*, etc.]

WILLI: You can't imagine how painful it was to me all night to watch him, turning and suffering and nothing I could do for him.

From the motion picture **Lifeboat.** Courtesy of Films Inc.-20th Century Fox.

KOVAC (John Hodiak): Why didn't you stop rowing?

WILLI: Why should I?

STANLEY (Hume Cronyn): To help him.

WILLI: The best way to help him was to let him go. I had no right to stop him, even if I wanted to. A poor cripple, dying of hunger and thirst—what good could—could life be to a man like that?

STANLEY: He was trying to tell me something. If I could only remember.

WILLI: He's better off now—out of his trouble.

STANLEY: Something about water.

ALICE (Mary Anderson): He was in agony from thirst. I wanted to cry, but the tears wouldn't come.

MRS. PORTER (Tallulah Bankhead): No, how could they? If I remember rightly, tears are water with a trace of sodium chloride. Isn't that so, Willi?

WILLI: Ja.

KOVAC: What about sweat? What's the chemical composition of sweat?

MRS. PORTER: Water—with a trace of something or other.

STANLEY: Now I remember! Gus said . . . Willi had some water.

JOE (Canada Lee): Yeah—right under his shirt.

WILLI: Quite so. I took the precaution of filling the flask from the water beakers before the storm. Just in case of emergency. And I had food tablets and energy pills too. Everybody on a U-boat has them. You should be grateful to me for having the foresight to think ahead. To survive one must have a plan. But there's nothing to worry about. Soon we'll reach the supply ship, and then we'll all have food and water. Too bad Schmidt ["Gus Smith"—Bendix] couldn't have waited.

ALICE: You—

(Voices)

JOE: Please don't—please, Miss Alice!

[They all, but Joe, attack and beat the Nazi and throw him overboard to his death]

RITTENHOUSE (Henry Hull): To my dying day I'll never understand Willi or what he did. First he tried to kill us all with his torpedoes—nevertheless we fished him out of the sea and took him aboard and shared everything we had with him. You'd have thought he'd've been grateful ... but all he could do was plot against us. Then he—he let poor old Gus die of thirst. What do you do with people like that? Maybe one of us ought to try to row. Where to? What for? No—when we killed the German we killed our motor.

JOE: No, we still got a motor. [He looks up to God]

RITTENHOUSE: Yeah? Who? Naw, we're through.

STANLEY (to Alice): Are you afraid?

ALICE: No; I don't think so.

STANLEY: If we had got out of it I—I was going to ask you to marry me. What do you think you'd have said?

ALICE: I think I would have said yes.

STANLEY: Well then, whatever happens, I'd like you to marry me.

MRS. PORTER (cynically): Congratulations. Well that's settled. And what now, little Men?

RITTENHOUSE: I've been a widower for eighteen years. We never had any children. All I'll have behind me are a great many millions of dollars. I hope they do somebody some good.

MRS. PORTER: So we're all going to fold up and die just because that ersatz superman's gone.

RITTENHOUSE: My only regret is that in the end I joined a mob.

MRS. PORTER: Baloney! We weren't a mob when we killed him. We were a mob when we sat around, prisoners of the man we'd saved—kowtowing to him, obeying him, practically heiling him because he was kind enough and strong enough to take us to a concentration camp! Good grief, look at you! Rittenhouse—C. J. Rittenhouse, self-made man. Made of what? As long as you're sitting there thinking up your last will and testament, I'll write your epitaph for you now—Ritt, he quit! That goes for you too, Narcissus [Kovac, she refers to his tatoo]—it's a good thing there's room on that chest of yours for another letter—Q for quitter. And you, Joe, it's all right for you to look up and trust in somebody, but how about giving Him a hand? What's the matter with us? We not only let the Nazi do our rowing for us, but our thinking. Ye gods and little fishes! Fishes. Ye god!

We haven't got energy pills but the ocean's full of the millions of fish swimming around. Well—why don't we catch some?

[They now proceed to try to save *themselves*—optimistically.

In the next scene they are about to be rescued after they watch a destroyer blow up a U-boat. Just before they are picked up they fish out a boyish-looking German from the wreckage.]

BOY: Oh, danke Schoen [Thank you]

ALICE: It's his arm. Let's get his coat off.

RITTENHOUSE: Hey, wait a minute. Have you forgotten about Willi already?

MRS. PORTER: But Ritt, this is different. The kid's wounded.

RITTENHOUSE: Throw him back.

MRS. PORTER: Don't be silly, darling, he's—he's helpless. He's only a baby.

KOVAC: The baby has a toy [uncovering a hidden gun].

JOE: I should have finished him.

RITTENHOUSE: You see? You can't treat them as human beings. You've got to exterminate them.

KOVAC: Easy, Ritt—he'll be taken care of.

BOY: (German) Werden Sie mich nicht umbringen?

MRS. PORTER: He says—aren't you going to kill me?

ALICE: I'll have to tie this up til the ship's doctor takes care of it.

KOVAC: [Mockingly, quoting the boy] Aren't you going to kill me! What're you going to do with people like that?

STANLEY: I don't know. I was thinking of Mrs. Higley and her baby—and Gus.

MRS. PORTER: Well maybe they can answer that.

End of film.

Mission to Moscow

James Agee
(May 22, 1943)

[The next review, by James Agee, who until his death in 1955 was this country's outstanding film critic, looks at another kind of war propaganda film, frankly and crudely political in intent and method. The film, *Mission to Moscow,* is Hollywood's sugar-coating of the American-Russian wartime alliance.]

Reprinted from *Agee on Film,* Vol. I. Copyright 1943 by the James Agee Trust. Published by Grosset & Dunlap, Inc.

As cinema and as warfare, *Mission to Moscow* is an important piece. Not entirely without skill, it inaugurates for a great general audience a kind of pamphleteering and of at least nominal nonfiction whose responsibilities, whose powers for good or evil, enlightenment or deceit, are appalling; and of which we are likely to get a great deal from now on. (Walter Huston touring Mr. Willkie's *One World* seems like a foregone conclusion.) This first film is likely to hasten and intensify our cooperation with the Soviet Union. It may even help frustrate those who—if my naive impression is correct—plan to win this particular peace by destroying the Soviet Union, dominating Europe with the help of Bryn Mawr graduates and domesticated democrats, and reducing China to an Anglo-American-owned, Japanese-policed laundry. To whatever degree the film may help frustrate such intentions, and enrich our alliance, I feel considerable passion in its favor. It will be the first time that moving pictures have even flexed their muscles in a human crisis. Aside from these purely practical issues, however, the picture fascinates me chiefly as a phenomenon. So does the question how it came to be made in the first place.

There are other questions. Did the government urge the film on Warner Brothers? Is it federally subsidized or lend-lease? Are the sacred treatment of the President and the adroit suggestion that all isolationists were Republicans parts of a deal or mere good-will? We can only suspect, through rumor and internal inference, that the Stalinists here stole or were handed such a march that the film is almost describable as the first Soviet production to come from a major American studio. Almost, but not quite. For it is indeed, as Manny Farber has well said, a mishmash: of Stalinism with New Dealism with Hollywoodism with journalism with opportunism with shaky experimentalism with mesmerism with onanism, all mosaicked into a remarkable portrait of what the makers of the film think that the American public should think the Soviet Union is like—a great glad two-million-dollar bowl of canned borscht, eminently approvable by the Institute of Good Housekeeping.

As such, it is as rich a subject for diagnosis as any other dream.

Up to a point—not far short of first base—it is serviceable. It is good to see the conservatives of this country, Great Britain, France, and Poland named even for a fraction of their responsibility for this war. It is good to see the Soviet Union shown as the one nation during the past decade which not only understood fascism but desired to destroy it, and which not only desired peace but had some ideas how it might be preserved and how it would otherwise inevitably be lost. It is good for that matter to hear even an oblique line spoken in favor of Basic English—a line by the way which underlines the rumor that Madame Litvinov played a strong hand behind-screen.

But that is about as much good as I can find, barring some sincere performances and some rather inchoate directorial nervous energy. The rest is shameful rot. Not that *Mission to Moscow* is either remarkably more true or more false than the characteristic reflexes of Hollywood, the press, the schools, the politicians, or civilization in general: simply, it indulges the all but universal

From the motion picture **Mission to Moscow.** Courtesy of Museum of Modern Art.

custom of using only so much of the truth as may be convenient and of regarding aesthetic integrity, human verisimilitude, and psychological credibility as scullions, dismissible without notice if employable at all. This sort of irresponsibility is insulting and inimical to its producers, appraisers, and consumers alike, and those who accept or excuse it insult and endanger themselves still again, from within. The immediate incidental pragmatic effect may be good. But the deeper effect is shame, grief, anaesthesia, the ruin of faith and conscience and the roots of intelligence; and the real end, as should be reasonably clear just now, is disaster.

Letting that be for the moment, what are some examples?

Mr. Davies himself is one in his prologue, indorsing the gospel truth of this production—a figure as much of dream as of reality. As a big business man, the figure which has replaced Lincoln as the American archetype, he is a creature whose wisdom, disinterest, reliability are final and above question.

The man whom Ambassador Huston faithfully calls "Boss" is another. Boss is here accorded almost the divine invisibility of "good taste" which Jesus Christ rated in Fred Niblo's *Ben Hur*, where a Mazda bulb stood in for the Nazarene; and his voice, even in intimate conversation with Joe, sounds as if he were telling a hundred and thirty million of his friends that we planned it that way.

Ambassador Huston is still another, as he carries his honest Tarkingtonian charm around brightest Russia, Seeing for Himself with an Open Mind. He sees little of the colossal country and the astonishing people Warner Brothers might at least have half tried to let him see. But Davies himself didn't see either, actually. He saw what ambassadors, officials see; and the film shows him doing just that, no more. This is one of the most faithful notes in the film really. What little Mr. Huston does see, however, will be mighty illuminating to those fifty million-odd moviegoers who have never had his advantages. For there is no essential difference, it turns out, between the Soviet Union and the good old U.S.A., except that in Russia everybody affects a Weber and Fields accent and women run locomotives and you get tailed by a pair of harmless comics who claim to be GPU men. The Ambassador learns this sort of good news in a series of dialogues on that "educational" radio level in which a mere scientist asks a Pasteur, "Just what *is* this H_2O, Doctor Coffee-Nerves?" and gets a wrong answer. Mrs. Davies and Madame Molotov, meanwhile, put on a woman's-page skit with a serving maid which makes Elinor Ames's *The Correct Thing* look like the correct thing. Later, at a "history"-making reception, two 'cello-voiced Soviet officials stroll past the camera with the most endearing Daisy Ashfordism in years. Commissar Cox opines, "We are entering a new era, don't you think so?" Commissar Box retaliates, feelingly, "*I* think we have done *remarkably well!*"

About the trials I am not qualified to speak. On surface falsifications of fact and atmosphere I might, but on the one crucial question, whether Trotsky and Trotskyists were or were not involved with Germany and Japan in a plot to overthrow the government and to partition the country, I am capable of no sensible opinion. I neither believe it nor disbelieve it. I neither believe nor disbelieve evidence to the contrary. I am unable to trust the politicians of either camp or of any other to supply me, the world in general, or even their closest associates, with the truth. I am unable to be sure, even, that men of such intelligence, courage, and integrity as Professor Dewey are undeceivable in such matters, deeply as I respect them; so I am unable, in turn, to be convinced by their findings and opinions. It may be that this painful impotence is an impotence merely of my own spirit; it may be that I am immobilized, rather, by my conviction that a primary capacity for telling or discovering the truth is possible, today, to few human beings in few types of occupation or allegiance. In any case I can attempt to learn the truth, and can defend, or attack, only in areas where I can rely in some small degree on the hope of emergent truthfulness in the material and in those who are handling it.

Why We Fight

Frank Capra

(1971)

[Another way in which Hollywood went to war was in using its human and technical resources in direct partnership with government agencies, particularly the military. Many of its top production and acting talent entered military service, as Frank Capra, a standout director for many years before and after the war, recounts in a chapter from his recently published memoir, *The Name above the Title.*]

It was difficult for me to keep up with Lyman Munson as he led me through the labyrinthian ways of the Pentagon. He was a hard driver, a jet-like man always ahead of his sound. In fact, just standing still Munson seemed to create a whirlwind. I'll never forget the way he put on his tunic, on the run. Grabbing its collar with both hands he would fling it high overhead, deftly let both sleeves slide down his upright arms—and the tunic was on without Munson losing his stride.

Lyman *had* to be on the run to act as warden, nurse, and Boy Scout leader to dozens of touchy civilian egos he had straitjacketed in uniforms: high and haughty Harvard professors who spoke to neither the Cabots nor the Lodges; mulish newsmen who thought "channels" were for greased swimmers; Madison Avenue ad men who stressed, "If the bottle is pretty enough you can sell sea water"; authors whose every word was gospel; and Hollywood "names" who wouldn't step on a carpet unless it was red.

And now Munson was escorting me to the office of the Chief of Staff. General George C. Marshall had sent for me. He wanted to talk to me alone. Not being a military man I didn't fully realize that this was tantamount to a private audience with the Pope.

We stopped at a hall door with the sign CHIEF OF STAFF over it. "Give your name to the guard inside, Frank. When he says go in, walk into Marshall's door without knocking. And *don't salute.* If he's busy, walk over to the chair at the right of his desk and sit down. Shoot straight, Frank, and with few words. See you."

Left alone I made for a nearby drinking fountain. But even water was a poor antidote for a cottony mouth. Suddenly I felt fear, homesickness—an uncontrollable urge to fly home to my family, to hide in the loving warmth of my wife and kids. But my feet wouldn't move, as they won't in a bad dream.

Officers passed me by without a glance; their faces drawn, unshaven. I leaned over the fountain, let the water cool my hot, dry lips. Then I walked to the door marked CHIEF OF STAFF.

Der Führer

Hitler we live

From the motion picture **Prelude to War.** Courtesy of Museum of Modern Art.

There he sat behind a desk, gray, spare, undistinguished, quietly checking off items on a list. "Don't salute!" Munson had warned. Had I tried I would have fallen flat on my face. Without moving his head his pale blue eyes flashed me a quick look. "Major Capra, sir," I heard my voice saying.

His eyes returned to his papers. Yep, I thought to myself, he could be cast as a sad-eyed Oakie watching his soil blow away. There was the chair at the right of his desk. I walked to it, sat on its edge, clamped cold clammy hands on my twitching knees—and waited.

I was impressed by the intense concentration of this quiet man; he seemed to give the blue-cone tip of his mind to each item he checked off. Scribbling something quickly, he turned to me, smiling faintly—but only with his eyes.

"Good morning, Capra. You know, it's a constant inspiration to realize how many of our fine minds are giving up careers and family life, and putting on uniforms. Yes, in a total dedication in this terrible emergency." His eyes held and searched mine. "And that's fine. That's America. Mr. Capra—allow me to call you that for a moment—you have an opportunity to contribute enormously to your country and the cause of freedom. Are you aware of that, sir?"

I knew my answer was important to him. But all I could blurt out was, "Well, General Marshall, I—I mean if you're asking me does it scare the heck out of me, I'll have to say, yessir. It does!"

The fine lines of a smile radiated from his straight mouth and joined the crinkles round his eyes. I knew I could fall in love with this man.

With utter frankness he talked for about an hour. He told me we were raising a very large army—around eight million—and that we were going to try to make soldiers out of boys who, for the most part, had never seen a gun. They were being uprooted from civilian life and thrown into Army camps. And *the reason why* was hazy in their minds.

"Within a short time," he said, "we will have a huge citizens' army in which civilians will outnumber professional soldiers by some fifty to one. *We* may think this is our greatest strength, but the high commands of Germany and Japan are counting heavily on it being our greatest weakness.

"Our boys will be too soft, they say, too pleasure-loving, too undisciplined to stand up against their highly trained, highly indoctrinated, highly motivated professional armies. They are sure the spirit, the morale of their individual soldier is superior to ours. He has something to fight and die for—victory for the superman; establishing the new age of the superstate. The spoils of such a victory are a heady incentive.

"Now, how can we counter their superman incentive? Well, we are certain that if anyone starts shooting at Americans, singly or collectively, Americans will fight back like tigers. Why? Because Americans have a long record of survival when their skins are at stake. What *is* in question is this: Will young, freewheeling American boys take the iron discipline of wartime training; endure the killing cold of the Arctic, the hallucinating heat of the desert, or the smelly muck of the jungle? Can they shake off the psychological diseases indigenous to all armies—boredom and homesickness?

"In my judgment the answer is 'Yes!' Young Americans, and young men of all free countries, are used to doing and thinking for themselves. They will prove not only equal, but superior to totalitarian soldiers, *if*—and this is a large if, indeed—they are given answers as to *why* they are in uniform, and *if* the answers they get are *worth* fighting and dying for.

"And that, Capra, is our job—and your job. To win this war we must win the battle for men's minds. Osborn and I think films are the answer, and that you are the answer to such films. Now, Capra, I want to nail down with you a plan to make a series of documented, factual-information films—the first in our history—that will explain to our boys in the Army *why* we are fighting, and the *principles* for which we are fighting."

"General Marshall, it's only fair to tell you that I have never before made a single documentary film. In fact, I've never even been near anybody that's made one—"

"Capra," he said, with a slight edge to his voice, "I have never been Chief of Staff before. Thousands of young Americans have never had their legs shot off before. Boys are commanding ships today, who a year ago had never seen the ocean before."

"I'm sorry, sir. I'll make you the best damned documentary films ever made."

He smiled. "I'm sure you will. We are all being asked to do what we never dreamed we could do. I'm asking you to tell our young men why they must be in uniform, why they *must* fight. These films are a top priority. I'll send you and Osborn a directive to that effect. Take charge as you have in Hollywood. Any serious hitches, report them back to me. Any questions?"

"Plenty, sir. But I'll find the answers," I said, rising. He gave me a sharp, quick look. "Thank you, Capra."

In his fleeting glance, before returning to his papers, the pale blue eyes of that quiet, severe man burdened with awesome power, revealed the loneliness of his soul—the constant yearning for guidance in the secret depths of those who must make decisions.

Leaving General Marshall's office I walked into a washroom to lock myself into a cubicle; to be alone; to think things out. The simple but enormous thrust of the assignment was bewildering. "Tell our young men *why* they are in uniform, *why* they must fight—" Yes, and why many will be blown to pieces. Always the young, the flower of youth. Did not Jehovah require young Isaac as a sacrifice from old Abraham?

I hadn't the foggiest idea of how to make a documentary film. To me, documentaries were ash-can films made by kooks with long hair. I was no expert on the reasons and causes of war. I had no organization, no money, no plan. But I did have a direct order from the Chief of Staff, and a desk in a small room with five other desks, and a painted sign: MAJOR FRANK CAPRA, ORIENTATION FILM SECTION. I was the section.

Shortly after General Marshall ordered me to make the *Why We Fight* films for our servicemen, I saw Leni Riefenstahl's terrifying motion picture, *Triumph of the Will.* The film was the ominous prelude of Hitler's holocaust of hate. Satan couldn't have devised a more blood-chilling super-spectacle.

Using the facilities of the Nazi-commandeered UFA film empire, Leni Riefenstahl (a woman producer) made the classic, powerhouse propaganda film of our times. It was at once the glorification of war, the deification of Hitler, and the canonization of his apostles. Though panoplied with all the pomp and mystical trappings of a Wagnerian opera, its message was as blunt and brutal as a lead pipe: We, the Herrenvolk, are the new invincible gods!

Triumph of the Will fired no gun, dropped no bombs. But as a psychological weapon aimed at destroying the will to resist, it was just as lethal.

The film's opening was a master stroke of god-building. In an aura of celestial music, an invisible, mystic camera photographed Hitler's invisible spirit descending toward earth from the clouds and stars of Valhalla, and gliding lower and lower over the beautiful German countryside.

As the messiah of malice brushed unseen wings over chimneytops, multitudes of waving, cheering, hysterical Nazis hailed the visitation with ovations of HEILS!—offering up the incense of bedlam in adoration of "his coming."

The music crashed out its *Götterdämmerung* to the gods of freedom; the supernal specter touched down on an airport runway; glided to a full stop; then—silence.

Magically, a plane door opened; its mystic frame dark with mystery. Then, god the spirit materialized into god the Führer—uniformed, resplendent, stigmatic with swastikas. He stepped forward, clicked his heels, blessed the chosen with the Nazi salute—and Thor loosed its thunderbolts. A Valkyrian roar of SIEG HEIL! ruptured the silence and rolled in thundering echos. The Nuremberg Congress of supermen had opened! A hundred thousand storm troopers—booted, armed, swastika-draped—stood rigid row on row, as Hate walked alone to his altar of microphones.

The Voice of Hate shrieked from millions of radios: "We are the master race!" "SIEG HEIL!" amened a hundred thousand throats. "Today, Germany! Tomorrow, the world!" "SIEG HEIL!"..."SIEG HEIL!"..."SIEG HEIL!"...

Then Hitler walked among his supermen who stood rigidly at attention. Blond, booted, helmeted Siegfrieds—swastika flags billowing—their faces shone with pagan madness as Hitler gripped each right arm in the warrior's clasp, forearm to forearm, and eyes met eyes in a wild hypnotic troth—vowing the blood oath of obedience.

Mass murder of innocents is beyond human understanding. But a viewing of *Triumph of the Will* should have predicted it—to any mind that could have remained unshriveled by horror.

Yes, the message of the film was plain and brutal: "Power is ours! Unbeatable power! Surrender, all ye weak babblers of freedom! The meek shall inherit only the earth to fill their graves. Surrender!"

That film paralyzed the will of Austria, Czechoslovakia, Scandinavia, and France. That film paved the way for the Blitzkrieg. That film practically paralyzed my own will as I walked slowly back to my battered desk to sit alone and unnoticed in a roomful of officers, each engrossed in his own inadequacies to meet the challenge of war.

I sat alone and pondered. How could I mount a counterattack against *Triumph of the Will;* keep alive *our* will to resist the master race? I was alone; no studio, no equipment, no personnel. Commandeering a Hollywood studio for this effort seemed out of the question. Could I plan idea films and turn them over to the Signal Corps for production? Did they have the creative brains to cope with such propaganda blockbusters as *Triumph of the Will?* No. The Signal Corps was geared to training films: how to fire machine guns, build trenches, clean rifles—the "nuts and bolts" type of visual aids to explain the "hows" of war, not the "whys." The struggle for men's minds was too new, too highbrow, too screwball for old-line colonels who still referred to soldiers as "bodies."

Earlier, I had dropped in on the poobah of Signal Corps films, Colonel Schlosberg, to tell him about my directive from the Chief of Staff. He was impressed, not with me, but with the growing importance of his film empire. Yessir! Producing films for the high command! He could visualize that new star, perhaps two stars, on each shoulder.

"Why that's fine! Fine!" he said, each word a heavy pat on my head. "See? I told you Morale was the right spot for you. You prepare the scripts, get them approved, then bring them over here to me. If I think they're feasible I'll give them a project number and forward them to Colonel Gillette in Astoria, Long Island."

I played it low key; pleaded, reasoned; appealed to his God, his country, the emergency. "Allow me to make just these *special* General Marshall films at Astoria. On my word, I won't interfere with any system you and Colonel Gillette have set up—"

"You bet your ass you won't. Because if I let *you* get away with it, every Tom, Dick, and Harry in the Army'll wanna come in to make their own films—medical, transportation, ordnance, what have you. No! Only the Signal Corps can handle or touch film. It's in our charter and nobody, but *nobody,* can change it. Not even your Chief of Staff."

Well, here we go again. Another battle against entrenched stupidity. "Colonel Schlosberg, I know this war is wrecking a lot of little sand castles. You should see what it did to mine. But you're in a civilian army, now. And all we civilians want is to get the hell out of uniform as fast as we can, nothing more. Now the Chief of Staff gave me an urgent job to do, and charters or no charters, *I'm going to do it.* Understand, Colonel? So why don't you cooperate before the going gets rough for all of us?"

"Are you trying to threaten a superior officer?"

"Oh, balls. No, sir. I'm the village idiot trying to save the neck of a superior officer."

Was it Fate that decreed that my life should be a continuous battle against the Establishment, in the Army as well as in Hollywood? Or was I creating my own environment in my obsession to become number one in any job I tackled? Was I building up Colonel Schlosberg into a villain that barred my way, a Goliath that had to be overcome—like Harry Cohn or L. B. Mayer? In fact, isn't Fate just the apothecary that fills out the life prescriptions we ourselves prescribe?

Did I *need* villains to do my thing? If there had been no Harry Cohns, or L. B. Mayers, or Colonel Schlosbergs in my life, would I have had to create them?

It would have been stupid, if not disloyal, to allow the inspirational *Why We Fight* films to be made by Signal Corps colonels to whom soldiers were "bodies"; colonels who were automatically hostile to the power of ideas; colonels dumb enough to have earlier refused to admit me to a "secret" showing of *Triumph of the Will* because *I was not yet cleared by "security."* The expert who was commissioned to fight enemy propaganda was not "cleared" to see an enemy propaganda film. No wonder dictatorships of *all kinds* are doomed to fail.

But more important than how or where I would produce answers to *Triumph of the Will* were the answers *themselves*. What *were* the answers? What *were* the antidotes to the poisonous ideas of a master race—be it blond or yellow?

I needed one basic, powerful idea, an idea that would spread like a prairie fire, an idea from which *all* ideas flowed. I thought of the Bible. There was one sentence in it that always gave me goose pimples: "Ye shall know the truth, and the truth shall make you free."

Did it also mean the truth would make you strong? Strong enough to stop Hitler and Tojo? What *was* the truth about this World War? Well, it was obvious to me that the Nazis of Germany, the warlords of Japan, and the Fascists of Italy were out to deliberately take over the free nations by force, so they could stamp out human freedom and establish their own world dictatorships. If that statement was the truth, free men everywhere would fight to the death against it.

But how did *I* know that statement was true? Who proved it to *me*? Why the enemy *himself* proved it to me, in his acts, his books, his speeches, his films.

That was the key idea I had been searching for—on my feet in Pentagon halls, on my back in bed, and on my knees in pews. Let the *enemy* prove to our soldiers the enormity of his cause—and the justness of ours.

Colonel Munson startled me out of my brown study by sitting on my desk and quipping that I was getting paler and paler since seeing *Triumph of the Will.* I assured him my paleness was nothing—inside I was getting greener and greener.

"Come on, Frank, you need some air. Let's go home and see what the wife's got for dinner."

In the car Lyman told me that General Osborn and General Surles, Army Public Relations head, had had some powwows with Lieutenant General Somervell, chief of G-4 (Service of Supply), about forcing the Signal Corps to cooperate in the production of Special Services films. The Signal Corps, Lyman said, had breathed dragon fire on the talks.

Munson also chewed me off for having given Pathe News in New York my personal check for three thousand dollars for the historical newsreel footage I had ordered because only the Signal Corps could buy film and they had disapproved buying it for me. So I was out three thousand clams. But he said he had approved my hiring of Edgar Peterson, a local Washington documentary film man, as a Civil Service assistant, and that I had permission to hire other film people as Civil Service employees.

Lyman Munson, a West Point general's son, and his wife, "Jimmy," a West Point general's daughter, lived in a small Army duplex in Alexandria, Virginia. Theirs was the typical barracks romance of army brats. Both were born and raised in army barracks. They met and fell in love in army barracks. And they got married and lived happily ever after in nothing but army barracks.

While Lyman Munson was mixing drinks and Jimmy Munson was conjuring up salivating smells in her kitchen, we were joined by Lyman's number two man, Jack Stanley, and his very beautiful wife. With them was—surprise!—a red-mustached American captain with a British accent; a Yorkshireman whose unruly shock of dark red hair seemed as full of mischief as his sharp, ferret-like eyes. He was Eric Knight, the author of *The Flying Yorkshireman,* the *Sam Small* stories, *This Above All,* and *Lassie Come Home.*

For me it was love at first sight with Eric Knight. He had all the talents that could be compressed into a single writer: Wit, compassion, sensitiveness, an intriguing style, and a great, great love for human beings. He had Keats's "mighty idea of beauty in all things." But this above all—Eric was a rollicking boon companion; one of the three most charming men I met in the service, the other two being his good friends novelist Paul Horgan and painter Peter Hurd.

After dinner, while the wives washed the dishes, the four of us—two West Point men, a noted British author, and a Hollywood film director, all American Army officers—talked about what we could never stop talking about: psychological warfare against paranoids who had, psychologically and on the field of battle, just about convinced many nations in the world, and a good many people in our own country, that it was useless, and perhaps senseless, to struggle against the power structure of the master-race trinity: Hitler-Tojo-Mussolini.

I told them of my hunch: Use the enemy's own films to expose their enslaving ends. Let our boys hear the Nazis and the Japs shout their own claims of master-race crud—and our fighting men will *know* why they are in uniform. Eric jumped to his feet. "Frank, if you never get another bloody idea you'll still be way ahead. It smacks of Thomas Aquinas's pet debating ploy; discuss all your opponents' main points—then powder them."

Munson and Stanley were equally enthusiastic. "Okay," I said, "but I've got to have a film set-up of my own. And more important, I need the enemy films. Who's got them all?" They looked blank.

"Lyman," I butted in, "I'll lay ten to one the Signal Corps is too dumb to think of grabbing up propaganda films. There's got to be a big cache of enemy newsreels somewhere, and with your permission I'm starting out at dawn on a one-man film hunt. And if I get my hands on any, I'm setting up my own film unit to make General Marshall's films, even if I have to make them in the broom closet I sleep in at the Carlton—room 308."

Jimmy Munson poked her head in the door to announce: "Lousy news on the radio, fellas. The Japs drove MacArthur's men off Bataan. They're holed up in Corregidor, the poor bastards. Anybody want a drink?" No answer. She withdrew to the kitchen.

"Frank, what if Schlosberg has already nailed down those enemy films?" asked Munson quietly.

"Aw, come off it, Lyman. Frank's got a rare champion spirit, man. Why don't we back him up? Sure, the Army snipers'll take pot shots at him. But you know bloody well the weapon isn't made that can shoot down ideas."

Eric Knight was to tragically prove his point in less than a year.

Edgar Peterson, a bright young ivy leaguer who knew his way around Washington's film alleys, was my first Civil Service employee. He increased the personnel of my film section by a whopping 100 percent. I really hired him to find me a place to store the thirty cans of nitrate (dangerously flammable) newsreel film I had bought (with my own money) from Pathe News. He said every dinky film-cutting room in Washington was rented, but he knew of a little-known government film set-up that was practically moribund. Only one problem—it belonged to Secretary of Interior Ickes, and Ickes was a hard man to shave. He took me to see it.

A square service building called the "Cooling Tower" stuck up in the middle of the inner court of the North Interior Building. It housed the heating and cooling machinery for Ickes's multistoried Department of Interior. But the first two floors were all occupied by Interior's 16 mm film set-up—cutting rooms, projection facilities and storage vaults. It also had two old-fashioned 35 mm projection machines. Obviously some of the privileged help saw movies there. We found two old Civil Service retainers trying to look busy. One, Mr. Dame, was the Chief; the other, Walter West, was obviously the Indian. They looked frightened as they watched an Army officer case their little empire. I told Pete to get a set of keys and set up a little office for us and make an inventory of the equipment. He was in the middle of inventory-taking when I walked into the Cooling Tower the morning after dinner at the Munson's and said: "Pete, you're a pretty good film hound. Bring your smeller and let's try to track some down."

We tried smelling for enemy films at the State Department. They sent us to the FBI, who sent us to the Treasury Department, who said, "Try the Alien Property Custodian," who referred us to Mr. Samuel Klaus, a special assistant to Treasury's General Counsel. The trail ended. For us, Samuel Klaus—a small, baldish Jew—was Santa Klaus.

"What can I do for you, Major?" he asked curtly, without rising.

"German and Japanese newsreels, Mr. Klaus."

"What about 'em?"

"General Marshall has asked me to make films that'll show our boys what kind of bastards they are fighting—and *why.*"

His eyes lit up. But his voice was still dry and flat. "Sit down, Major. Or should I call you Mr. Deeds or Mr. Smith?" I bowed and gratefully sat down. "Yes, Frank Capra, I've got *warehouses full* of German and Japanese films; all their newsreels for the past twenty years. But you're a few days late. Here's a request from the Chief Signal Officer to turn all this film over to the Signal Corps."

My heart almost stopped. "Mr. Klaus, I'm talking to you now as one American citizen to another. Telling our soldiers why they are being drafted has got to be our number one priority. If these enemy films get buried in Signal Corps channels it'll take me months just to get to see them. I need these films *now.*"

He looked at me for a long time as he pulled on his lower lip. Then he leaned forward on his desk and said: "Frank Capra, are you telling me that you, an Army officer, handed me a formal written request *five days ago,* asking the Alien Property Custodian to deliver all enemy films in his possession to you, for the purpose of making information films for the Army at the direction of the Chief of Staff—"

Peterson and I walked away on air. We had found the great cache of enemy films—and it was ours! Now to officially get the Cooling Tower. We ran to it, barged in, and announced to the old retainer that the Army was commandeering half of his quarters to store important Army films.

I raced to Temporary Building H to tell Munson and Osborn of our good fortune—leaving out the pre-dating part to avoid implicating them in any official conspiracy. Munson said: "Nice going." General Osborn, a man of character, was worried. His Special Services Division had no right to accept the responsibility for such films. I reminded the General that I had signed for the films personally and as a Signal Corps officer, and not in the name of his Special Services.

The good general was still worried; he abhorred gutter-type infighting. But I was no gentleman. I hated war; hated to dignify it with rules of conduct. I hated being a second-class citizen; hated having to get an okay to make a long-distance call, or send a telegram; hated having to remain within fifteen minutes of Washington without an approval from the Adjutant General—which took about five days. I hated having to swallow the galling figment that someone else's opinion was superior to mine because he outranked me. But I hated becoming a slave of a master race even more. At least my wife and children were free. And I would resort to the dirtiest kind of infighting to keep them free. So come Army charters, or clod-pated colonels, or gentlemen generals, I would make films that justified this war to our soldiers.

The final confrontation took place in a small conference room in Special Services' new quarters in the Pentagon. In a private meeting demanded by them, a livid Colonel Schlosberg and a very uncomfortable Colonel Darryl Zanuck, ¹·ınded me an official ultimatum: "Turn over all films in your name to the Chief Signal Officer, or face court-martial. And that's a direct order from the Chief Signal Officer."

I told them exactly what they could do with their ultimatum *and* the Chief Signal Officer; reminded them that I was given a direct order from the Chief of Staff to make the *Why We Fight* pictures. And that if I was stupid enough to turn that responsibility over to pompous asses like Colonel Schlosberg, I deserved to be shot, not court-martialed.

I warned the Colonel to stop trying to bury me, because whether he liked it or not, in the world of film—in Hollywood, in the Army, or in the toilet— wherever I sat was the head of the table. And if he didn't believe it, he should ask Darryl Zanuck about the contract his Twentieth Century-Fox company offered me, which I turned down to join the Army.

They left, making dire threats—against Special Services as well as me.

Munson and Osborn were deeply concerned about this inter-Army jurisdictional squabble. They thought I should go to General Marshall about it. I said the Chief of Staff was too busy running a global war. Besides, he had said, "Capra, take charge." I urged General Osborn to take the offensive against the

Signal Corps; accuse, protest, challenge. If that didn't work I could always scrounge enough equipment from my friends. And we could always hire more civilian personnel. I already owned the Cooling Tower and its measly equipment. They said I *didn't* own the Cooling Tower. The Secretary of the Interior could throw me out anytime. I pointed out that Ickes wouldn't dare. There's a war on! And anyway, what with the mountains of captured film I had in the Cooling Tower, Ickes wouldn't have enough trucks to throw me out.

It all began to sound like comic opera—"The Great Celluloid War" between the Know-It-Alls of Hollywood and the Got-It-Alls of Pentagon—while MacArthur's men died inch by inch at Corregidor.

And then—the unexpected and unfunny happened. It murdered our confidence. When my seven writers (volunteer Hollywood civilians) turned in their treatments—each had been assigned a segment of the historical decade between Manchuria and Pearl Harbor—I was aghast. The outlines were larded with Communist propaganda.

I huddled with Osborn, Munson, and Watrous. They were shocked. Special Services was already in difficulty with the Congressional Appropriations Committee; the chairman was suspicious about orientation films for the Army. "What the hell is this 'orientation' business—a new word for propaganda?" If the slightest hint were leaked to the Committee that the scripts contained pro-Communist stuff—Zap! Our necks would be out a mile, and the Signal Corps was waiting with the ax. The outlines were classified "top secret" and the writers were quietly dismissed.

We all realized the project was so sensitive it could only be carried out with controllable men in uniform. General Osborn must ask for power to enlist and commission his own film personnel, or ask that his Special Services Division be relieved of the responsibility for carrying out General Marshall's directive. Quiet waters run deep. Gentle General Osborn gave me a lesson in high-class infighting. On May 2, 1942, a memo directing the Chief Signal Officer to "establish a Signal Corps (film) Detachment under the Jurisdiction and Direct Control of the Chief of Special Services," went out from the Office of the Commanding General, Services of Supply—namely, Lieutenant General Somervell.

The 834th Photo Signal Detachment was born. Jubilation reigned. I immediately signed a year's lease on a large house in Bethesda, and phoned Lu to bring the children and Rosa the cook and Kelly the nurse.

Meanwhile, Anatole Litvak, Tony Veiller, Robert Heller, and Leonard Spiegelgass (pending their induction into the Army) and I went to work on the *Why We Fight* scripts, on which we would base the following seven fifty-minute "must see" one-hour training films (ten minutes allowed for filling and emptying theaters):

1. *Prelude to War*—presenting a general picture of two worlds; the slave and the free, and the rise of totalitarian militarism from Japan's conquest of Manchuria to Mussolini's conquest of Ethiopia.

2. *The Nazis Strike*—Hitler rises. Imposes Nazi dictatorship on Germany. Goose-steps into Rhineland and Austria. Threatens war unless given Czechoslovakia. Appeasers oblige. Hitler invades Poland. Curtain rises on the tragedy of the century—World War II.

3. *Divide and Conquer*—Hitler occupies Denmark and Norway, outflanks Maginot Line, drives British Army into North Sea, forces surrender of France.

4. *Battle of Britain*—showing the gallant and victorious defense of Britain by Royal Air Force, at a time when shattered but unbeaten British were only people fighting Nazis.

5. *Battle of Russia*—History of Russia; people, size, resources, wars. Death struggle against Nazi armies at gates of Moscow and Leningrad. At Stalingrad, Nazis put through meat grinder.

6. *Battle of China*—Japan's warlords commit total effort to conquest of China. Once conquered, Japan would use China's manpower for the conquest of *all* Asia.

7. *War Comes to America*—Dealt with who, what, where, why, and how we came to be the U.S.A.—the oldest major democratic republic still living under its original constitution. But the heart of the film dealt with the depth and variety of emotions with which Americans reacted to the traumatic events in Europe and Asia. How our convictions slowly changed from total non-involvement to total commitment as we realized that loss of freedom anywhere increased the danger to our own freedom. This last film of the series was, and still is, one of the most graphic visual histories of the United States ever made.

These were the seven *Why We Fight* films that were to revolutionize not only documentary filmmaking throughout the world, but also the horse-and-buggy method of indoctrinating and informing troops with the truth. Primarily made by the Army for the Army, they were used as training films by the Navy, Marine Corps, and Coast Guard. The British, Canadians, Australians, and New Zealanders used them as training films for their armed forces. Translated into French, Spanish, Portuguese, and Chinese they were shown to the armed forces of our allies in China, South America, and in various parts of Europe and Africa.

One film was shown to the American people in theaters. By an order from Winston Churchill *all* were shown to the British public in theaters. The Russians showed *Battle of Russia* throughout all their theaters. And in the chaotic months of occupation after the war, American Embassies played the *Why We Fight* series in enemy countries, charging ten cents for admission. The State Department has stated that these showings enriched our treasury by more than $2,500,000—a sum six times greater than their original cost.

Thus, the *Why We Fight* series became our official, definitive answer to: What was government policy during the dire decade 1931–41? For whenever State, the White House, or Congress was unable, or unwilling, to tell us what our government's policy had been (and this happened often) I followed General

Marshall's advice: "In those cases make your own best estimate, and see if they don't agree with you later." By extrapolation, the film series was also accepted as the official policy of our allies.

Thus, it can be truly said that the *Why We Fight* films not only stated but, in many instances, actually created and nailed down American and world pre-war policy. No, I won't say it. Yes, I will say it. I was the first "Voice of America."

About May 10, 1942, Mrs. Capra came to Washington with her brood: Frankie (eight), Lulu (four), Tommy (one), and Rosa the cook and Kelly the nurse. We moved into a two-story, four-bedroom house in Bethesda, Maryland, surrounded by a spacious lawn and large black-trunked trees. And surprise! We all saw our first fireflies and just couldn't believe them. The kids put them in bottles and, squealing with excitement, used the bottles as sparkling flashlights to explore the house and garden with.

The fireflies were delightful—but not the servants' quarters in the concrete basement: two ugly, cramped, uncarpeted cubicles shot through with exposed steam and sewer pipes—designed with malice to keep the Negro in his place. In fact, I was informed that most houses around Washington were all magnolia and Southern hospitality upstairs and all skunk cabbage and bigotry in the cellar.

I moved out of room 308 at the Carlton, but refused to give it up. For the next four years it would be my sometime home and tiny eddy of quiet in the Washington millrace for the scores who came to work for us a few hours or a few days. Even while living in 308 I allowed others to use it in the daytime. Some days as many as three shifts of sleepers occupied the room. Visiting wives kept trysts with uniformed husbands. Visiting celebrities like John Gunther or Charles MacArthur simply asked Frank Swazey, the hotel manager, for a key and shacked up with me for a day or two.

Leonard Lyons wrote this item about room 308 in his New York *Post* column:

> Marc Connelly will write a movie for Frank Capra's film-division of the Army . . . Connelly reported for work in (congested) Washington. In Capra's office he met Kurt Weill, the composer, and Maxwell Anderson, the playwright . . .
>
> "Capra was thoughtful enough to reserve a little room for me," Connelly told Weill. "Were you able to get a reservation, Kurt?" . . . "Yes," the composer replied, "I'm in Room 308, at the Carlton." "But that's the room I'm in," said Connelly, "and I suppose that bag I saw in the corner of the room was yours." . . . "No, it isn't," Weill added. "That bag is Maxwell Anderson's."

Playwright Charles MacArthur, now Major MacArthur, an aide to the commanding general of the hush-hush Chemical Warfare Service, had never been a fan of my films. Too corny for that hard-nosed ex-reporter. But as we hit the sack in room 308 one night, he poked me with a stubby finger and asked: "I want to know something. My general told me a guy by the name of Capra did a helluva piece of research at Caltech twenty-five years ago: Spontaneous combustion of liquid carbon disulfide saturated with silicon-hydride gas, to burn holes in enemy masks. Was that you?" "Charlie! You speak the lingo good—" "Was that *you*?" I nodded. He pumped my hand. "You're nothing but a goddam Dago, you know that?" he said, and turned off the light.

Room 308, unlisted and unrentable, was exactly seven feet wide and twelve feet long. But it had a three-quarter bed, an open clothes closet, a three-drawer bureau below an oval mirror into whose wavy glass one could look darkly and see mysterious sunsets. And it had one chair, and one dirty screened window which tamed the zeal of the sunniest day into the anemia of twilight.

One person could negotiate the obstacle course of boots, bags, bed legs, and Peter Hurd's guitar without breaking toes—if he wore his shoes. Two persons had to walk sideways like crabs. If a third person came in, traffic was paralyzed. But at times we were as many as eight, sprawled on the bed and wedged on the floor, shouting in bull sessions, or listening to Peter Hurd, Paul Horgan, and Eric Knight sing folk songs. And a delight it all was for my next-door neighbor, wise old Barney Baruch, who occasionally—when he wasn't advising F.D.R. and Cabinet members, or sitting in a park trading Socratic ironies with fellow bench warmers—joined our goings on. Room 308. A broom closet. But never such a wonderful broom closet.

And now the Cooling Tower had figuratively shrunk to another broom closet. Much like hungry viruses invade a bacterium and multiply by eating their host, Edgar Peterson and I had invaded the Cooling Tower and multiplied into the 834th Photo Signal Detachment of eight officers and about twelve enlisted men. All were Hollywood professionals—directors, writers, and film editors. In addition, some twenty civil service personnel performed various duties.

Working like disciplined and tightly packed ants we attacked the making of the *Why We Fight* series. One group of translators (supplied by Iris Barry, film curator of New York's Museum of Modern Art, and by Army intelligence) rephrased the German and Japanese films into English. Another group catalogued and cross-filed the film scenes—a tedious, back-breaking job. Our main group worked on research and the scripts.

As the executive producer I outlined the scope and thrust of each of the seven fifty-minute films. Tony Veiller and I did most of the script-writing, although we had considerable help from some fair writing talent, namely, authors Eric Knight and James Hilton, screen writers Alan Rivkin and Leonard Spiegelgass, and newsmen William Shirer and Bill Henry.

At the very outset I assigned teams of assistant producers, writers, film editors, and research men to work more or less concurrently on each film. But the truckloads of impounded enemy film came rolling, came rolling, until there was no room at Ickes' Inn for even one team.

Furthermore, Paul Horgan would soon need a shooting crew for his *Officer's Candidate School* script, and Undersecretary of War Patterson was pressuring us for a Negro film to buck up the morale of our black soldiers. The Undersecretary put me in touch with his Negro adviser, Truman Gibson. Gibson opened up a thick dossier of sickening acts of discrimination against Negro troops in the South. Exaggerated? The Secretary of War didn't think so. There were too many reports equally incredible. He ordered Special Services to give the highest priority to a Negro soldier film, and assigned us a young Negro writer, Carlton Moss, to collaborate on the script.

Besides these urgent outside requests, I was anxious to launch my *Army-Navy Screen Magazine* and another series of orientation films: *Know Your Ally, Know Your Enemy.* So I asked permission to move the film section to Hollywood where we belonged in the first place. Osborn and Munson agreed—especially if I could also find a set-up for Tom Lewis's Armed Forces Radio which desperately needed the broadcasting talent and facilities on the West Coast.

Before my wife had finished unpacking at our rented house in Bethesda, I told her to start packing again while I rushed out to Hollywood for help. And I knew exactly who to go to for help—Colonel Darryl Zanuck. Zanuck knew my situation. He had been present when Schlosberg threatened me with a court-martial.

The old Western Avenue Twentieth Century Studios had been abandoned years ago. It was now a pile of run-down buildings—a ghost studio. I asked Darryl to let me have it for my film section and for Tom Lewis's Armed Forces Radio. He said, "Of course, it's all yours." He'd have it cleaned up and painted for me.

There was a Signal Corps procurement office in Hollywood. I officially requested that office to furnish and equip my new base on Western Avenue. Request turned down.

I quietly contacted friendly back-lot department heads in various studios; asked for any worn-out furniture and equipment they could spare. They dug me up old typewriters, desks, chairs, filing cabinets, and even old Movieolas and cutting-room tables and bins.

That sub-rosa operation "scrounge" moved George Stevens to join our unit. He was shooting a picture at Columbia Studios when he spotted me on one end of a beat-up desk that Ray Howell (Head of Props) and I were lifting into a studio truck. I was in uniform. "Frank! What in hell are you doing here, moving furniture?" "Sh-h-h. Make out you don't know me. I'm stealing this stuff." "You? You need an old desk? I though you were chief of something." "George, in the Army you've gotta be an Indian to get something done." "Well, Frank, I'm part Indian. Can you use me?" "My God, yes. Come over to Western Avenue. The old Fox studio—"

George Stevens came over. He was a major before he could raise his hand and say "How!" He asked to head a group of combat photographers. He did. In Europe until after the surrender.

The only equipment I couldn't "borrow" were sound projection machines. Old 35 mm projectors were at a premium because the military had priority on the new ones. So I ordered the two vintage projectors at the Cooling Tower to be secretly torn out of their concrete bases and shipped West to our new headquarters. We also practically shanghaied the Cooling Tower's civil service projectionist, Walter West, because Walter was the only man in the world that could coax the old machines to work. Since the projectors were non-synchronizing, he would run *picture film* on one machine and *sound track film* on the other, keeping picture and sound in sync by braking one machine or the other with his thumbs.

The whole *Why We Fight* series, the *Know Your Ally, Know Your Enemy* series, the *Army-Navy Screen Magazine, The Negro Soldier in World War II* were all made in that falling-apart borrowed studio with scrounged furniture and equipment, and those two horse-and-buggy projection machines we hijacked from Interior that had to be kept in sync with braking thumbs.

In wartime one learns to get around the lead-tailed colonels who squat on empires. In our case necessity was not a mother but a distressed maiden who brought many additional professional Hollywood knights to her rescue—in uniform: Anatole Litvak, Tony Veiller, John Huston, George Stevens, Willie Wyler, Sam Briskin, William Hornbeck, Leonard Spiegelgass, Merrill White, William Claxton, William Lyon, Henry Berman, Ted Geisel, Claude Binyon, Carl Foreman, Stu Heisler, David Miller, Bill Mellor, Joe Biroc, Joe Valentine, Eric Knight, and Meredith Willson and his great Santa Ana Air Force orchestra. And out of uniform: Walter Huston, Lloyd Nolan, Robert Stevenson, Bill Henry, Robert Flaherty, James Hilton, Alan Rivkin, Joe Sistrom, Edgar Peterson, Dimitri Tiomkin, Alfred Newman, plus the sound, music, and dubbing departments of Twentieth Century-Fox, Paramount, MGM, and (of utmost importance) the personal talents of Walt Disney and his best animators in making our animated maps artistic as well as informative.

The war information films were made in spite of the heavy-handed opposition of entrenched colonels. They had warehouses full of unwrapped equipment and facilities to spare. But we had the brains, the talent, and the desire. With these, and our industry's cooperation on a no-profit—often on a no-cost—basis, Hollywood professionals made film history in a field strange to them—documentary films, the private preserves of intellectuals.

In October, 1942, just three years after I took *Mr. Smith* to Washington and was run out of town, I took another picture to Washington for its premiere showing: *Prelude to War.*

General Osborn described the Chief of Staff's reaction to our first *Why We Fight* film, in a letter Osborn wrote to Lu:

Dear Mrs. Capra:

Your husband's film, *Prelude to War,* was shown to General Marshall yesterday . . . When the lights went on there was complete silence in the room for two minutes or more. Then General Marshall turned, looked about until he saw your husband and said, "Colonel Capra, how did you do it, that is a most wonderful thing." Then he called him over and talked about it part by part in detail with him. . . . It was a moving occasion. . . .

(signed) F. H. Osborn

The day the White House showing of *Prelude* was scheduled General Marshall invited me to lunch alone with him in his office. He was most friendly and most pleased that his idea of troop information films had started so auspiciously with *Prelude to War.* He asked me if all the film was authentic. I said it was. Our only re-creations were newspaper headlines and, of course, the animated expository war maps. He asked where the enemy film came from. I told him I had possession of all German, Japanese, and Italian newsreels made in the last twenty years. And also most of their propaganda documentaries made before and during the war.

Then he wanted to know how I obtained the film. "General Marshall, it's a long, boring story. Point is, I've got all the captured enemy film, I'm negotiating for Russian war film, T. Y. Lo of the China News Agency has promised me all their Chinese film, and Donovan's O.S.S. is stealing current enemy newsreels for me in border countries . . ."

I was hoping he wouldn't bring up the next subject, but he did. "Osborn has hinted that you've had problems with the Signal Corps. Have you?" "No real problems, sir." "Frank, these *Why We Fight* films are of enormous value, for us and for our allies. Any delays from any source—and you come direct to me." "General Marshall," I said jokingly, "I'll make you a deal. I'll let you stick to winning the war, if you let me stick to minding the film store."

He grinned. He liked people who knew they could get things done. He then said Secretary Stimson wanted to make certain that all policy statements made in *Prelude to War* had been checked for accuracy. "Have they?" he asked. I answered that all policy questions had been checked with State, OWI (Office of War Information), and Presidential advisers such as Lowell Mellett. To most questions we got clear-cut answers; to some, elliptical answers or none at all. On these matters my staff and I stood back and did what the General himself had advised: made the best objective guesses as to what our policies had been.

Again he beamed at my answer, and said he would have Osborn run the films for State, OWI, and for congressional leaders. Only then did it dawn on me just how far General Marshall was sticking his neck out in having the Army make information films (propaganda his detractors would call them) for captive Army audiences. Only his great faith in the belief that free men are better fighting men when they are well informed could make this great soldier step into a political and psychological arena where civilian angels feared to tread.

In the next couple of years I was to enjoy many such talks with General Marshall, especially during dinners with him alone at the Chief of Staff's house, "Quarters Number One," the large, comfortable, two-story red-brick building at Fort Myer, Virginia, across the Memorial Bridge. Only a Filipino enlisted cook would be with the General. Between seven and seven thirty we would have two stiff, bourbon old-fashioneds which the Chief liked to mix himself.

There would be talk of course, but absolutely no war talk. That day he probably had had to make decisions that affected the fate of nations; tomorrow he would face problems equally crucial. But that evening he would be calm and unworried as he listened to my chatting. Once, I asked him how he stood up under the strain; he answered: "I've had to train myself never to worry about a decision once it's made. You worry before you make it, but not after. You make the best judgment you can about a problem—then forget it. If you don't, your mind is not fit to make the next decision."

At exactly seven thirty the Filipino would serve dinner at a small table, and for the next hour and a half I would answer questions about all the techniques of motion pictures: acting, photography, sound recording, animated cartoons, musical comedies. Or, I would tell him about my early years, or Papa's green thumb; how he could make mature orange tree limbs grow roots, then saw them off and present them to friends as full-bearing orange trees; how he sprinkled ground-up minerals around the roots of rose bushes and changed the colors of the roses.

And when he found out I owned a large fruit ranch he wanted to know all the details, and being a compost buff himself, he flipped his top when I described to him our large concrete compost pits and the machinery for making and turning the compost. This in turn would inspire the General to talk in glowing terms about his Dodona Manor in Leesburg, Virginia, where he hoped to retire and plant all kinds of fruits, vegetables, and flowers. And I would plead with him not to use any poisonous sprays.

His eyes shone as he spoke of working with soil. But they shone brightest when he talked of his experiences in commanding CCC boys' camps in Florida and the Pacific Northwest. For in those camps he first met the frail, anemic, poverty-stricken youths of the Great Depression. In those camps he first decided to bring young men back to health, courage, and manhood through education—feeding the mind as well as the stomach—teaching them to acquire abilities that would make the most of their born-with capacities.

It was his experience with the CCC boys that led him to conceive and add a new and revolutionary concept to the American Army—a Morale Division which catered to the welfare of the mind and soul of a soldier. For the first time a heart was implanted into a military system that had referred to service men as "bodies" and "numbers." One result of that new concept: the *Why We Fight* series of Army information films. Another result: my lasting friendship with one of the great men of our century, George Catlett Marshall.

To those who knew and loved G.C.M., it was no accident that Chief of Staff Marshall, the architect of military victory in Europe, should, as Secretary of State Marshall, be the architect of the Marshall Plan to help Europe recover from "hunger, poverty, desperation, and chaos." Nor did it surprise us when he was honored with the Nobel Peace Prize.

So Proudly We Fail

James Agee

(*The Nation,* October 30, 1943)

We suffer—we vaguely realize—a unique and constantly intensifying schizophrenia which threatens no other nation involved in this war. Geography is the core of the disease. Those Americans who are doing the fighting are doing it in parts of the world which seem irrelevant to them; those who are not, remain untouched, virginal, prenatal, while every other considerable population on earth comes of age. In every bit of information you can gather about breakdowns of American troops in combat, overseas, even in the camps, a sense of unutterable dislocation, dereliction, absence of contact, trust, wholeness, and reference, in a kind and force which no other soldiers have to suffer, clearly works at the root of the disaster. Moreover, while this chasm widens and deepens daily between our fighting and civilian populations and within each mind, another—much deeper and wider than any which geography alone could impose—forms and increases between this nation and the other key nations of the world. Their experience of war is unprecedented in immediacy and unanimity. Ours, even in the fraction which has the experience at all, is essentially specialized, lonely, bitter, and sterile; our great majority will emerge from the war almost as if it had never taken place; and not all the lip-service in the world about internationalism will make that different. This, and more and worse, is all so obvious, so horrifying, and so apparently unalterable that, being a peculiarly neurotic people, we are the more liable to nod and pay it the least possible attention. That is unfortunate. Our predicament is bad enough as it stands; the civil and international prospect is unimaginably sinister.

Since it is beyond our power to involve ourselves as deeply in experience as the people of Russia, England, China, Germany, Japan, we have to make up the difference as well as we can at second hand. Granting that knowledge at second hand, taken at a comfortable distance is of itself choked with new and terrible liabilities, I believe nevertheless that much could be done to combat and reduce those liabilities, and that second-hand knowledge is at least less dangerous than no knowledge at all. And I think it is obvious that in imparting it, moving pictures could be matchlessly useful. How we might use them, and how gruesomely we have failed to, I lack room to say; but a good bit is suggested by a few films I want to speak of now.

Even the Army Orientation films, through no fault intrinsic to them, carry their load of poison, of failure. You can hear from every sort of soldier from the simplest to the most intricate what a valuable job they are doing. But because they are doing it only for service men they serve inadvertently to widen the abyss between fighters and the civilians who need just as urgently to see them. Civilians, however, get very little chance to learn anything from moving pictures. We are not presumed to be brave enough. And the tragic thing is that after a couple of decades of Hollywood and radio, we are used to accepting such deprivations and insults quite docilely; often, indeed, we resent anyone who has the daring to try to treat us as if we were human beings.

Just now it is a fought question whether numbers four and five of the Orientation Series, *The Battle of Britain* and *The Battle of Russia,* will get public distribution. Whether they do depends on what is laughingly called the Office of War Information and on what is uproariously called the War Activities Committee. The OWI's poor little pictures, blue-born with timidity from the start, have finally been sabotaged out of existence; and judging by the performance to date of the WAC, it is not very likely that we shall see these films. And if we do see them, it is more than likely that we shall see them with roast albatrosses like *The Keeper of the Flame* hung around their necks.

I can only urge you to write your Congressman, if he can read. For these films are responsible, irreplaceable pieces of teaching. *Britain,* one hour's calculated hammering of the eye and ear, can tell you more about that battle than you are ever likely otherwise to suspect, short of having been there. *Russia,* though it is a lucid piece of exposition, is cut neither for fact nor for political needlepoint but purely, resourcefully, and with immensely powerful effect, for emotion. It is by no means an ultimate handling of its material, but it is better than the Russian records from which it was drawn, and next to the tearful magnificence of *The Birth of a Nation* is, I believe, the best and most important war film ever assembled in this country.

Beside it Samuel Goldwyn's *The North Star* is something to be seen more in sorrow than in anger and more in the attitude of the diagnostician than in any emotion at all. It represents to perfection some crucially symptomatic characteristics of Hollywood and of the American people in so far as Hollywood reflects, or is accepted by, the people. Hollywood's noble, exciting, all but unprecedented intention here is to show the conduct of the inhabitants of a Russian border village during the first days of their war; to show real people, involved in realities, encumbered by a minimum of star-spotlighting or story. The carrying out of that intention implies in every detail the hopeless mistrust in which Hollywood holds its public. To call this "commercial" and to talk about lack of intelligence and taste is, I think, wide of the main mark. The attitude is more nearly that of the fatally misguided parent toward the already all but fatally spoiled child. The result is one long orgy of meeching, sugaring, propitiation, which, as a matter of fact, enlists, develops, and infallibly corrupts a good deal of intelligence, taste, courage, and disinterestedness. I am sorry not to talk at length and in detail about this film. I can only urge you to watch what happens in it: how every attempt to use a reality brings the romantic juice and the annihilation of any possible reality pouring from every gland. In its basic design Lillian Hellman's script could have become a fine picture: but the characters are stock, their lines are tinny-literary, their appearance and that of their village is scrubbed behind the ears and "beautified"; the camera work is nearly all glossy and overcomposed; the proudly complicated action sequences are stale from overtraining; even the best of Aaron Copland's score has no business ornamenting a film drowned in ornament: every resourcefulness appropriate to some kinds of screen romance, in short, is used to make palatable what is by no remote stretch of the mind romantic. I think the picture represents the utmost Hollywood can do, within its present decaying tradition, with a major theme. I am afraid the general public will swallow it whole. I insist, however, that that public must and can be trusted and reached with a kind of honesty difficult, in so mental-hospital a situation, to contrive; impossible, perhaps, among the complicated pressures and self-defensive virtuosities of the great studios.

The thing that so impresses me about the nonfiction films which keep coming over from England is the abounding evidence of just such a universal adulthood, intelligence, and trust as we lack. I lack space to mention them in detail (the new titles are *I Was a Fireman, Before the Raid*, and, even better, *ABCA* and the bleak, beautiful, and heartrending *Psychiatry in Action*), but I urge you to see every one that comes your way. They are free, as not even our Orientation films are entirely, of salesmanship; they are utterly innocent of our rampant disease of masked contempt and propitiation. It comes about simply enough: everyone, on and off screen and in the audience, clearly trusts and respects himself and others.

There is a lot of talk here about the need for "escape" pictures. To those who want to spend a few minutes in a decently ventilated and healthful world, where, if only for the duration, human beings are worthy of themselves and of each other, I recommend these British films almost with reverence as the finest "escapes" available.

FOR DISCUSSION

1. On the basis of reading the reviews, compare the earliest efforts at American film propaganda during World War I to the mass persuasion commercial films of World War II. To what extent were the World War II films influenced by (and structurally improved because of) the Soviet and Nazi examples of the twenties and thirties?

2. In 1940, Canadian film expert John Grierson wrote again of his faith in the Western world—particularly America—to produce "democratic" propaganda films. He saw the World War II era as the time when propaganda could serve the cause of humanity. Consider his comments as you read through all of the material on the American movies of World War II (and, hopefully, screen some of them). Had American propaganda lived up to Grierson's standards? Compare his comments of 1940 to those of critic James Agee, who in 1943 analyzed the nature of such films during the course of the war.

3. Of all of the American pre-war preparedness films, none generated more controversy than Time-Life's *The Ramparts We Watch*. After reading all of the criticism (and, hopefully, screening the film), evaluate the film's one-sided interpretation. Considering the onslaught of Nazi aggression in 1940, was the film's theme justifiable? Was its use of out-of-context extracts from the German *Baptism of Fire* any more ethical than the fright-provoking content of *Baptism of Fire* itself? (According to the Time-Life publicity on *Ramparts* . . . the Nazi footage was confiscated and provided by John Grierson. Does the resulting propaganda film violate Grierson's democratic principles on this subject?)

4. Alfred Hitchcock's *Lifeboat* tried to stimulate anti-Nazi sentiment by portraying the German U-Boat captain as the cunningly evil intellectual superior to the American and British survivors who've "captured" him. *New York Times* critic Bosley Crowther adamantly objected to this "super-human" portrayal of an enemy. After reading Crowther's critique, the film producer's defense, and the screenplay extract, comment on the propaganda value of such a film. Does it achieve the persuasive goals the producer claims, or does it, as Mr. Crowther indicates, backfire?

5. Once a reader comes to terms with Frank Capra's name-dropping and self-inflating, there's a lot of fascinating information about the workings of the military (no different from any mass bureaucracy) and its wartime collaborator, Hollywood. The *Why We Fight* films were just as good as Frank Capra says that George Marshall said they were. (Even James Agee, who assigned to the garbage dump anything with the slightest smell of phoniness, wrote approvingly of the series.) Screen at least one (hopefully more) of the films and discuss your experience of it in the light of Grierson's hopes for propaganda, Agee's misgivings, and the flak over *The Ramparts We Watch* and *Lifeboat*.

6. The only example of a humorous treatment of propaganda included in this book is Charlie Chaplin's *The Great Dictator,* but humor has often been one of the propagandist's most effective weapons. What do you think are the strengths and weaknesses of using humor as a propaganda tool?

PART FOUR

The Cold War

In the years following World War II, the United States discovered that she had a "new" powerful enemy. The Soviet Union under Josef Stalin, a temporary ally during the war, proved to be a militant aggressor in Eastern Europe. In the Far East, the rise to power of the Chinese Communists (then considered in the Russian camp), and the Nationalist-Communist civil war in Korea dictated a fierce anti-Communism in American foreign policy. The late forties and early fifties were the years of myopic internal investigations in the United States, designed to purge the country of any disloyal (i.e., pro-Russian) elements. The controversial House Un-American Activities Committee (HUAC) investigated the nation's mass media, claiming they had been infiltrated with Communists and were clandestinely being used for "Red" propaganda. Hardest hit by these investigations was the motion picture industry. Several actors, writers, and directors were accused as Communists, and ten men were actually jailed for being in contempt of Congress for refusing to answer the Committee's questions.

Following the investigations, Hollywood yielded to political pressures by expelling any artists or technicians whose loyalty was the least bit suspect. A series of secret blacklists was circulated, designed to bar from the industry virtually anyone who voice opposition to HUAC's hearings.[1] By the early 1950s, with the ascendancy of Senator Joseph McCarthy (whose name has labeled the era) as the nation's number one "Red baiter," the country was in the grips of a self-conscious "Red scare." Now that the "enemy" had been ferreted out, Hollywood, anxious to make amends for allowing "leftists" in its ranks (and for producing all those pro-Russian films during the War), began making a series of new propaganda films which were all fiercely anti-Communist. Films like *I Was a Communist for the FBI, The Conspirator, My Son John,* and *Big Jim McLain* attempted to propagandize national conformity to patriotic norms by portraying Communism as a deadly evil.

As you read through this section, which is composed of reviews and screenplay excerpts from the anti-Communist films, keep the following factors in mind. First of all, note the similarity of the Communist or Russian agents in these films to the movie-Nazis of the World War II era. In virtually every case, they are simply one-dimensional "bad guys." Many of the same actors even play the villains in both types of films.

---

1. For complete details on these investigations and their impact, see Walter Goodman, *The Committee* (N.Y.: Farrar, Straus and Giroux, 1968), pp. 207–225.

From the motion picture **Point of Order.** Courtesy of Museum of Modern Art.

Secondly, imagine the embarrassment of Hollywood executives, who as part of their patriotic duty during the War produced all of those pro-Soviet films like *Mission to Moscow* and *Song of Russia.* After HUAC's investigation, with the radical change in the country's international mood and policy, film industry leaders must have felt the need to make amends quickly.

Finally, these films (with the exception of *I Was a Communist for the FBI*) were critical and box-office failures. Unlike their World War II counterparts, these cold war epics were simply not very popular, though both types of films were cut from exactly the same mold. This raises an interesting question concerning the nature of cinematic propaganda: To what extent does national mood condition the effectiveness of propaganda?

At the conclusion of this section, film critic Pauline Kael evaluates a typical cold war movie, *The Night People,* and compares it to one of the few concentrated efforts at Communist propaganda on film produced in this country, *The Salt of the Earth.* In her essay, she offers several insights on why the films of this era failed as propaganda.

I Was a Communist for the FBI

Bosley Crowther

(*The New York Times,* May 3, 1951)

I Was a Communist for the FBI, screen play by Crane Wilbur, based on the story of Matt Cvetic, as told to Pete Martin; directed by Gordon Douglas; produced by Bryan Foy for Warner Brothers. At the Strand.

Matt Cvetic	Frank Lovejoy
Eve Merrick	Dorothy Hart
Mason	Philip Carey
Jim Blandon	James Millican
Crowley	Richard Webb
Gerhardt Eisler	Konstantin Shayne
Joe Cvetic	Paul Picerni
Father Novac	Roy Roberts
Harmon	Eddie Norris
Dick Cvetic	Ron Hagerty
Garson	Hugh Sanders
Ruth Cvetic	Hope Kramer

Twelve years ago, Warner Brothers let loose a hot and lurid blast at Nazi agents in this country with their *Confessions of a Nazi Spy.* Now they are blasting Communist agents with equal fervor and alarm in a hissing and horrendous spy film called *I Was a Communist for the FBI.* Based on the magazine memoirs of Matt Cvetic, a Pittsburgh steel worker who actually did some sleuthing for the Federal bureau as a "plant" in a Communist cell, this film is an erratic amalgam of exciting journalistic report, conventional "chase" melodrama, patriotic chest-thumping and reckless "red" smears. Riding a wave of public interest, it opened at the Strand yesterday.

In many respects, this heated item bears comparison to the hearings before the House Un-American Activities Committee—which, incidentally, it extols. For in telling its story of a valiant patriot who silently endures the contempt of his son, his brothers and his neighbors while he poses as a loyal Communist, it tosses off dangerous innuendos and creates some ugly bugaboos in the process of sifting the details of how the Communists bore from within.

For instance, in glibly detailing how the Communists foment racial hate and labor unrest in this country, it colors its scenes so luridly that the susceptible in the audience might catch a hint that most Negroes and most laborers are "pinks." It raises suspicion of school teachers by introducing one as a diligent "party member" at the outset. (After she meets the hero and falls for him, she breaks away.) And, all the way through, it drops suggestions—always from the villains' oily tongue—that people who embrace liberal causes, such as the Scottsboro trial defense, are Communist dupes.

It is true that the writing, the acting and the direction of this film are in a taut style of "thriller" fiction that the perceptive will recognize. The villains are absolute rascals, so slyly and sneeringly played by James Millican, Eddie Norris and others that you wonder how they'd fool anyone. The first time we see them, they are guzzling champagne and eating caviar at a reception for Gerhardt Eisler in a fancy suite in a Pittsburgh hotel. In reply to the surprised observation of the fellow who turns out to be from the FBI, a comrade, far in his cups, proclaims lightly, "This is the way we're all going to live when we take over the country!" That gives you an idea of the menacing sort they are.

Likewise, Frank Lovejoy, who muscularly plays the title role, is a model of tight and efficient resolution, ingenuity and spunk. He is in easy contrast to the handsome, serious and infallible young men of the FBI. Dorothy Hart is pretty and conventional as the decent American school teacher who has swallowed the Communist line but who makes her escape, with the hero's assistance, when the comrades get wise to them. Roy Roberts is familiarly four-square as a wise and compassionate Catholic priest, Paul Picerni is tense as the hero's brother and Ron Hagerty is mawkish as his son.

All of these "good ones" fit neatly the standard patterns of loyalty, and the film itself glows with patriotism. But it plays a bit recklessly with fire.

I Was a Communist for the FBI,
Scene from Final Shooting Script

Screenplay by Crane Wilbur, based on the story of Matt Cvetic, as told to Pete Martin. (Matt Cvetic has been an FBI undercover "Red" for 9 years. He is about to give evidence before the House Un-American Activities Committee.)

255. Close Shot. Matt at the Table Facing His Questioners.
FIRST CONGRESSMAN'S VOICE: Are you a member of the Communist Party of America?
MATT: I have been a member for nine years. My party card is in your possession.
256. Close Shot. Blandon, Harmon, Massonovitch seated among spectators. They are surrounded by other members and sympathizers. Matt's reply startles them.
FIRST CONGRESSMAN'S VOICE: What was your purpose in joining the Party?
257. Close Shot. Dick Cvetic and Joe Cvetic seated among the spectators.
MATT'S VOICE: I joined it as an undercover agent for the Federal Bureau of Investigation—I was what is commonly known as a "plant."

As this comes over, both Joe Cvetic and the boy, Dick, react in stunned amazement.

258. Full Shot.

The reaction of the spectators, a growing hum of excitement culminating in a roar of anathema from the Commie section.

259. Group Shot. Blandon, Harmon, Massonovitch, these three staring at Matt in shocked silence, as their sympathizers, seated around them howl "Traitor— stool pigeon—fink—a Lousy Informer!" Quickly this group is surrounded by officers who silence them ad lib.

260. Med. Shot. Matt and the Questioning Congressman.

The Congressman refers to a pile of thick scripts which are on the table in front of him.

FIRST CONGRESSMAN: Do you recognize these volumes, Mr. Cvetic?

MATT: Yes, sir. Those are copies of the daily reports I made to the FBI.

CONGRESSMAN: Please give us a brief resumé of what you learned about the Communist Party.

MATT: I learned chiefly that its political activity is nothing more than a front. That it is actually a vast spy system, founded in this country by the Soviet, and composed of American traitors whose only purpose is to deliver the people of the United States into the hands of Russia as a colony of slaves. . . .

Dissolve to:

261. Close Shot. Matt as he nears the end of his testimony.

MATT: . . . the idea of Communism as common ownership and control by the people has never been practiced in Russia and never will be. Their State Capitalism is a Fascist horror far worse than the one Hitler intended for the world. That great liar of all times spoke the truth when he warned that there was a more dangerous Hitler to the East!

262. Full Shot.

As Matt concludes his testimony and walks up the aisle toward the back of the room, there is a storm of applause, punctuated by the boos and hisses of the Commies.

Father and Son — and the FBI

Robert Warshow

(1955)

Many Americans find themselves baffled and exasperated by that "anti-anti-Communism" which sees in over-vigorous efforts to expose the Communist menace a growing threat to American freedom no less dangerous than Communism itself. Their bewilderment is understandable, for such an equation is clearly absurd and too often conceals a desire to remain "neutral" in the struggle against Soviet totalitarianism. But the fear of an irresponsible anti-Communism does not come entirely out of thin air; there *is* a wrong way, a dangerous way, to be anti-Communist. Those who do not believe this may find it illuminating to see Leo McCarey's new film, *My Son John,* an attack on Communism and an affirmation of "Americanism" that might legitimately alarm any thoughtful American, whether liberal or conservative.

The film opens on a "typical" American town of the kind that certain Hollywood directors could probably construct with their eyes shut: a still, tree-lined street, undistinguished frame houses surrounded by modest areas of grass, a few automobiles. For certain purposes it is assumed that all "real" Americans live in towns like this, and, so great is the power of myth, even the born city-dweller is likely to believe vaguely that he too lives on this shady pleasant street, or comes from it, or is going to it. Church bells are ringing, and a "typical" American family—named Jefferson, in fact—is preparing to go to church. Two sons of the family, in army uniforms, stand before the house with their father, tossing a football back and forth; the mother is late in getting ready, and there is a good deal of "healthy" kidding about this. She comes out at last—a worn, tense woman, considerably out of key with her robust husband and sons, but playing up to their image of her—and the family drives off. It is the last day of the boys' leave, and they will soon be off to Korea; under the emotional weight of this fact, the Jeffersons behave as if they are carrying out some formal ritual of affirmation, trying to pack into every speech and gesture some complete statement of what they are and what they believe, very much like one of those advertisements in which some large corporation attempts with half a page of mawkish copy to set down "as a public service" the meaning of America. The mother in particular is treated as if she were the American flag or a familiar passage from the Declaration of Independence, ostentatiously *not* accorded any deference precisely because she is valued so profoundly and completely.

We learn soon that there hangs over this American family a shadow more menacing than the Korean War. The eldest son, John, a brilliant and rising young government official (already one's suspicions are aroused), has failed to get home

Reprinted from *The Immediate Experience* by Robert Warshow with permission from Paul Warshow.

From the motion picture **My Son John.** Courtesy of Museum of Modern Art.

to say good-bye to his brothers. When he does appear on the scene after they have left, he is a figure to fill any ordinary human being, let alone any red-blooded American, with loathing: pompous, supercilious, as sleek and unfeeling as a cat, coldly contemptuous of his father, patronizing to his mother; also, though nothing is said of this, one feels that he might be a homosexual. In fact, as will eventually be revealed, he is a Communist and a traitor, but at first there are only his father's truculent suspicions and his mother's half-acknowledged fears. Here, it may be said, the film does for a time present a "typical" American drama that is also something more than "typical"—it is real. Nothing is more characteristic of our fluid society than the process by which children so often become alienated from their parents, going beyond them in education and social status until the parents, who may have made great sacrifices to accomplish precisely this result, find themselves excluded from the triumph they have prepared, obliged to content themselves with taking a generalized pride in a child whose achievements they are perhaps not even equipped to understand.

This situation, agonizing for both parent and child, has the elements of tragedy, for it is full of guilt, and yet no one is to blame. But if this conflict of generations is to become the material of serious drama, the eye that sees it must retain a certain compassionate detachment and not itself be subject to the hallucinations that afflict the contending parties. In *My Son John*, the conflict is presented so naked and intense that it takes on the quality of a nightmare. Against the monstrous son—Robert Walker's characterization is essentially the same as in *Strangers on a Train*, where he played the role of a pathological murderer—there is set a father no less monstrous, a pillar of the American Legion presented as so outrageously bigoted, so hopelessly benighted, that one fails to understand why the Legion has not organized a boycott of the film, unless it be out of a truly selfless concern for freedom of expression. This father is principal of the local elementary school, where, as he informs us, he is engaged in teaching little children the "simple, down to earth" fundamentals of morality and Americanism. He has also been making a serious study of the problem of Communism, and he expresses his understanding of that problem in a song that is worth quoting in full:

> *If you don't like your Uncle Sammy*
> *Then go back to your home o'er the sea,*
> *To the land from where you came,*
> *Whatever be its name,*
> *But don't be ungrateful to me!*
> *If you don't like the stars in old glory,*
> *If you don't like the red, white, and blue,*
> *Then don't act like the cur in the story,*
> *Don't bite the hand that's feeding you!*

The son responds to this piece of folk poetry with icy-delicate feline mockery—a beautiful bit of acting—creating an almost heroic tension and raising for a short time the hope that out of the unalleviated enmity between father and son, over-stylized though it may be, will come some serious dramatic examination of the way each blind intolerance feeds on its opposite and is mirrored in it. One suspects, even, that just such a counterpoint was for a while intended by the makers of the film.

But if they had such an intention, they found themselves unable to sustain it. For between the struggling titans of unreason there is only the suffering mother, drawn out almost transparently thin by the pull of the contending forces—in most ways a psychologically true portrait, though presented by Helen Hayes with a mad jerky passion that affects one like a prolonged scratching on taut silk, but not at all the figure that is needed to make sense of the complex issues. For her there is no understanding, but only pain, and when the dreadful truth about her favorite son is no longer to be denied, she can do nothing but sink back definitively into the arms of her husband: since he was right about this, it follows that he has been right about everything. Farewell to the mistaken values that made her send her son to college, farewell to the risks of intellectual curiosity and broad humanitarianism and individual thinking: these things made her son a Communist spy, whereas her husband, who despised such things, is an anti-Communist; in her husband's stupidity will be her peace.

For in the end we are left in no doubt: what is being upheld is, precisely, stupidity. All through the film no effort is spared to emphasize the limitations of the father's thinking and his hatred and contempt for the mind; this image of him is built up deliberately and with considerable skill. I have already quoted the father's most sustained expression of political documents. He also—this educator!—refers to Communists as "scummies." He makes a big show of being unable to remember the name of his son's beloved professor (something "foreign," no doubt), spits when he witnesses an affectionate greeting between the two, and worries about his son's falling into the company of "those intellectuals I've read about." In one of the climactic episodes, exasperated by the son's cool superiority, he hits him with a Bible and then goes out to get drunk, returning late at night to mouth some more of his "simple, down to earth" ideas while he can hardly stand up. And all this we are to regard, not as an excusable want of intelligence, but as a higher form of wisdom; we are to admire the father for his sincerity and his faith—qualities, it is implied, which are inseparable from muddleheadedness and incoherence, which indeed *equal* muddleheadedness and incoherence, just as in those "public service" advertisements about America the special virtues of our tradition turn out to reside less in the ideas the ads set forth than in the disjointed stammer which the copy writer conceives to be the natural accent of the man in the street. "You've got more wisdom than all of us," Lucille Jefferson says to her husband, "because you listen to your heart." It is clear that listening to your heart means not using your head. And John Jefferson, after he has repented of his crimes (for no apparent reason) and been murdered by his former comrades, explains in a recorded posthumous confession that corruption first entered his soul when he began to respond to ideas and think for himself, forsaking "the only authorities I ever knew—my church and my father and mother." At the time of this confession, John is about thirty years old; we have seen what the "authority" of his parents amounts to. Besides, though this may be blasphemy, there are fathers—yes, and mothers too—who are Communists.

But John has spoken also of the authority of his church. This brings us to one of the most important and most disturbing elements of the movies. The Jeffersons are Roman Catholics, and Leo McCarey has before this been quite successful with what might be called "popularizations" of Catholicism, most notably in *Going My Way*. But if, as I have suggested, a thoughtful member of the American Legion might take little comfort in this film's "Americanism," a thoughtful Catholic might likewise find good reason to be disturbed at its Catholicism. Indeed, though some sections of the Catholic press welcomed the film, at least two leading Catholic periodicals, *America* and *Commonweal*, have criticized it severely.

The main thing to be said is that religion exists in this film only as a form of window-dressing, an essentially empty symbol to be counterposed occasionally to the symbols of Communism. Just as the elder Jefferson uses the family Bible to hit his son when he feels frustrated in argument, so the idea "religion" is used throughout the film as a kind of blunt instrument to settle every difficulty without resolving it. The film opens with the ringing of church bells, and it ends with John Jefferson's parents going into a chapel to pray for their dead son. But these elements are never realized in cinematic terms; they are presented so perfunctorily, so much as a matter of mere ideological decoration, that they have no strength as screen images—and, of course, in a movie it is not the intrinsic worth of an idea that counts, but the power with which it is made into an image; in the movie theater, we think with our eyes.

There is also a priest, played by Frank McHugh, but he is presented as an ineffectual and slightly comic figure, bustling about occasionally in the background on parish affairs but never permitted to enter the action. This treatment of him may have been quite deliberate, designed to make him harmlessly appealing to non-Catholic audiences (like the foxy-grandpa priest played by Barry Fitzgerald in *Going My Way*, or the boys' counselor type played by Bing Crosby). But the result is that the moral authority of the church, to which the film finally appeals, simply does not show. One cannot imagine going to Frank McHugh for help with a serious problem, and in fact the elder Jeffersons never think of discussing their difficulties with him. He exists merely as one of the film's "properties," like the car or the house. At the same time, as Nathan Glick has remarked in a review of the film in *Commentary*, the function of the priest is taken over by an agent of the FBI. It is he who gently and lovingly brings Lucille Jefferson to an understanding of the situation and leads her to see her moral duty; it is he who urges upon John Jefferson the release of confession; it is he who pronounces what is in effect John's funeral oration. And where the priest is fussy, shallowly cheerful, a little shrill, the FBI man is dignified, serious, warm, full of understanding and wisdom—in short, a figure of profound moral authority, a priest, one might say, of the secular law. Perhaps I need not labor the significance of this transfer of the priestly function to a police agency, but it should be remarked that one of the signal virtues of the real FBI has been its refusal to assume such a role.

Finally, there is an element of falsity in the film's whole conception of Communism that deserves some mention. It is true, as we know, that the Communists are members of a conspiracy, and that this conspiracy is ready to employ almost any means to achieve its ends. But the conspiracy is a political one, its characteristic crimes are political, and its characteristic weapon, in the United States at this time, is much more often a mimeograph machine than a gun. When John Jefferson is killed by a burst of gunfire from a long black sedan, the event may not in itself be impossible, but as an image on the screen it falls too easily into a familiar pattern, the pattern of the gangster film. It is easy to see why a movie director would be tempted to follow that pattern, but it impedes understanding. Communists are not like gangsters; they are usually more complex and their lives are much duller. In their own way, they are often the epitome of stodgy respectability (think of Alger Hiss, for instance). The melodrama—it is true, there *is* a melodrama—is buried deep below the surface, perhaps too deep to be brought up where it can be photographed.

With the character of John Jefferson himself, perhaps, one does occasionally get a sense of that depth: in his monumental self-satisfaction, in his way of using certain opinions and attitudes like dead mechanical counters in his secret game of "history," testifying to the frozen rigidity of his mind and spirit. But one essential element is lacking: the subterranean fire of fanaticism. Without that, one cannot wholeheartedly believe in John Jefferson as an adequate representation of the Communist; it is as if he had picked up his Communism as another man might pick up a love of chamber music, simply as part of his cultural furniture (there are such Communists, of course, but they do not become spies). The fact is that Leo McCarey is not enough of an artist to imagine why anyone might become a Communist, what inner needs of the personality might be served. Of course, he is not alone in this failure: even the explanations of ex-Communists are curiously inadequate. But the result is that he must fall back on easy clichés—for example, that Communism comes from "substituting faith in man for faith in God"—and thus, though he succeeds in making John Jefferson the most interesting figure in the movie, the character remains finally fragmentary and unrealized. Perhaps this may account in part for the unrelieved violence of the doctrine that this film expounds. The hidden logic seems to be: since we cannot understand Communism, it is likely that anything we cannot understand is Communism. The strongest and clearest image that one takes away from the film is that of the father, and his message is that we must fear and hate the best potentialities of the human mind.

Morality Plays Right and Left

Pauline Kael

(1954)

ADVERTISING: NIGHT PEOPLE

Ads for men's suits show the model standing against a suspended mobile. But the man who buys knows that the mobile doesn't come with the suit: it's there to make him feel that the old business suit is different now. The anti-Sovietism of *Night People* serves a similar function. But the filmgoer who saw the anti-Nazi films of ten years ago will have no trouble recognizing the characters in *Night People,* just as ten years ago he could have detected (under the Nazi black shirts) psychopathic killers, trigger-happy cattle rustlers, and the screen villain of earliest vintage—the man who will foreclose the mortgage if he doesn't get the girl. The Soviet creatures of the night are direct descendants of the early film archetype, the bad man. Those who make films like *Night People* may or may not be privately concerned with the film's political message (the suit manufacturer may or may not be concerned with the future of wire sculpture); in the film politics is period décor—used to give melodrama the up-to-date look that will sell.

Night People is set in Berlin: a U.S. soldier is kidnaped; he is rescued by a U.S. Intelligence Officer (Gregory Peck) who knows how to deal with the Russians. They are "head-hunting cannibals" and must be treated as such. The film is given a superficial credibility by documentary-style shots of American soldiers, by glimpses of Berlin, and by the audience's knowledge that Americans in Europe have in fact been kidnaped. One might even conceive that someone who understood the nature of Communism might view certain Communists as "cannibals." But it would be a mistake to confuse the political attitudes presented in *Night People* with anything derived from historical understanding. Nunnally Johnson, who wrote, directed, and produced the film, has referred to it as "Dick Tracy in Berlin." His earlier anti-Nazi production *The Moon is Down* could be described as "Dick Tracy in Norway," and many of his films could be adequately designated as just plain "Dick Tracy."

Actual kidnapings have posed intricate political and moral problems. Should the victim be ransomed by economic concessions, should a nation submit to extortion? Were some of the victims observers for the U.S. and where does observation stop and espionage begin? We know that our government must have espionage agents in Europe—can we believe in the innocence of every victim? If they were guilty of some charges but not guilty of all the charges, what kind of protest is morally possible? The drama in the case of a Robert Vogeler or a William Oatis is in the fathoming of moral and political ambiguities. While purportedly about an East-West kidnaping, *Night People* presents a crime and a rescue. The hero has righted the wrong before we have even had a chance to explore our recollections of what may be involved in political kidnapings. Soviet ambitions and intrigue become a simple convenience of the film maker: the label "Communism" is the guarantee that the hero is up against a solid evil threat. For the sake of the melodrama, the Communism cannot be more than a label.

Night People is not much worse or much better than a lot of other movies—they're made cynically enough and they may, for all we know, be accepted cynically. David Riesman has pointed out that nobody believes advertising, neither those who write it nor those who absorb it. And the same can be said for most of our movies. Somebody turns the stuff out to make a living; it would seem naive to hold him responsible for it. In a state of suspended belief a writer can put the conflict of East and West into the capable hands of Dick Tracy: the film wasn't really written, it was *turned out.* And the audiences that buy standardized commodities may be too sophisticated about mass production to believe films and advertising, but they are willing to absorb products and claims—with suspended belief. Audiences don't believe, but they don't *not* believe either. And when you accept something without believing it, you accept it on *faith.* You buy the product by name. Who would *believe* in *Rose-Marie?* Yet the audience, after taking it in, emerges singing the Indian Love Call and it becomes a substantial part of American sentimental tone. Who would believe that *Night People* presents a political analysis? Yet the political attitudes that don't originate in political analysis become part of national political tone. Acceptance is not *belief,* but acceptance may imply the willingness to let it go at that and to prefer the accessible politics (to which one can feel as cynical and "knowing" as toward an ad) to political thought that requires effort, attention, and involvement.

The bit players who once had steady employment as S.S. guards are right at home in their new Soviet milieu; the familiar psychopathic faces provide a kind of reassurance that the new world situation is not so different from the old one (we beat these bullies once already). Perhaps *Night People* can even seem realistic because it *is* so familiar. The make-believe that is acted out often enough attains a special status: it becomes a real part of our experience. (Films like *Quo Vadis, The Prisoner of Zenda, Showboat, The Merry Widow* have been made so many times that to the mass audience they have the status of classics; are they not immortal if three generations have seen them?) Advertising, using the same appeals—the familiar with the "new" look—also depends upon repetition to make its point. If we *believed* an advertising claim, hearing it once would be enough. It is because we do not believe that advertising uses repetition and variation into infinity to get its claims accepted.

The suggestion that politics as used in melodrama is advertising décor is not intended metaphorically. I wish to suggest that films (and other forms of commercial entertainment) are becoming inseparable from advertising, and that advertising sets the stage for our national morality play.

Advertising has been borrowing from literature, art, and the theater; films meanwhile are taking over not merely the look of advertising art—clear, blatant poster design—but the very content of advertising. Put together an advertising photograph and a movie still from *How to Marry a Millionaire* (another Nunnally Johnson production)and they merge into each other: they belong to the same genre. The new young Hollywood heroine is not too readily distinguishable from the model in the Van Raalte ad; if the ad is a few years old, chances are this *is* the same girl. In a few months she will be on the front of movie magazines and on the back of news magazines endorsing her favorite cigarette. She is both a commodity for sale and a salesman for other commodities (and her value as one depends upon her value as the other). In any traditional sense, Gregory Peck is not an actor at all; he is a model, and the model has become the American ideal. Advertising dramatizes a way of life with certain consumption patterns, social attitudes and goals, the same way of life dramatized in films; films are becoming advertising in motion. . . .

The common aim of attracting and pleasing the public has synthesized their methods and their content. The film and the ad tell their story so that the customer can take it all in at a glance. They show him to himself as he wants to be, and if flattery is not enough, science and progress may clinch the sale. The new toothpaste has an activating agent; new shirts and shorts have polyester fibers running through them; *Night People* is filmed in CinemaScope with Stereophonic Sound. Can we balk at technical advances that "2000 years of experiment and research have brought to us"? New "technical advances" increase not only the physical accessibility of cultural goods, the content of the goods becomes increasingly accessible. The film's material has been assembled, the plot adapted; sound engineers have amplified the hero's voice, and the heroine's figure has been surgically reconstructed (actresses who scorn falsies can now have plastic breasts built-in). The new wide screen surrounds us and sounds converge upon us. Just one thing is lost: the essence of film "magic" which lay in our imaginative absorption, our entering into the film (as we might enter into the world of a Dostoyevsky novel or *Middlemarch*). Now the film can come to us—one more consummation of the efforts to diminish the labor (and the joy) of imaginative participation.

All this has been done for us; all that's left for us is to buy. Suppose an audience does buy a film—what do they do with it? The audience is not exactly passive, it has its likes and its dislikes and expresses them—in terms drawn more from advertising, however, than from art. The audience talks freely about the actor's personality, the actress's appeal, the likableness of their actions. Film critics become experts in "craftsmanship" and mechanics; Dreyer's *Day of Wrath* is considered impossibly slow and dim, while *Night People* is found to be "racy," "well-made," and "fast-paced"—praise more suitable to the art of a Studebaker than to the art of the film. A patron who wanted to mull a Hollywood film over for a while would be judged archaic—and rightly so. There is nothing to mull over: a trained crew did all that in advance.

Melodrama, perhaps the most highly developed type of American film, is the chief vehicle for political thought in our films (*Casablanca, Edge of Darkness, To Have and Have Not, North Star*). Melodrama, like the morality play, is a popular form; structurally melodrama is the morality play with the sermons omitted and the pattern of oppositions issuing in sensational action. Its intention is primarily to entertain (by excitation) rather than to instruct (entertainingly). Labels stand for the sermons that are dispensed with, and the action is central.

In some of the war and postwar films the writers and directors seemed to feel they were triumphing over Hollywood and over melodrama itself by putting the form to worthwhile social ends: they put sermons back in. The democratic messages delayed and impeded the action, of course, but they helped to save the faces of those engaged in the work. . . . While the hypocrisy of the method made the films insulting and the democratic moralizing became offensive dogma, the effort did indicate the moral and political disturbances, and the sense of responsibility, of the film makers. *Night People* reduces the political thought to what it was anyway—labeling—and nothing impedes the action. The film is almost "pure" melodrama. The author doesn't try to convince himself or the public that he's performing an educational service or that the film should be taken seriously. The cynicism is easier to take than hypocrisy, but it also shows just how far we are going.

Heroism is the substance of melodrama, as of standard westerns and adventure films, but there is little effort in Hollywood to make it convincing or even to relate it to the hero's character (in *Night People* a few additional labels—the hero went to a Catholic college, he was a professional football player—suffice). We have come a long way since the days when Douglas Fairbanks, Sr., winked at the audience as he performed his feats; now the audience winks at the screen.

The political facts of life may shatter the stereotypes of Hollywood melodrama but economic facts support them. The formula hero-defeats-villain has been tested at the box office since the beginning of film history and it may last until the end. Melodrama is simple and rigid and yet flexible enough to accommodate itself to historical changes. The hero is always the defender of the right and he is *our* representative. He rarely changes labels; on the few occasions when he is not an American he demonstrates that those on our side are just like us. (Gregory Peck's first screen role was in *Days of Glory:* as a heroic Soviet soldier he fought the evil Nazis.)

The villains are marked by one constant: they are subhuman. If the hero of *Night People* did not know that the enemy are cannibals, he might feel some qualms about the free dispensation of strychnine (he must feel as sure as Hitler that those opposing him are beyond reconciliation). Film melodrama, like political ideology with which it has much in common, has a convenient way of disposing of the humanity of enemies: *we* stand for humanity; *they* stand for something else. The robbers who are shot, the Nazis who are knifed—they are cowards or fanatics and they don't deserve to live. Fear, on the one hand, and, on the other, devotion to a "misguided" cause to the disregard of personal safety are evidence of subhumanity. The villains are usually more expressive than the heroes because their inhumanity is demonstrated precisely by the display of extreme human emotions. (Gregory Peck, who is always a hero, is rarely called upon to register any emotion whatever. The devil can be expressive, but the hero is a stick of wood.) The villains are not human; if they were, they'd be on our side. When historical circumstances change and our former enemies become allies, we let bygones be bygones and they are restored to human estate. Thus the little yellow bastards are now cultured Japanese; the blood-guilty Germans are now hardworking people, so akin to Americans in their moral standards and ability to organize an efficient economy; now it is the Russians, the courageous pioneers and fighting men of the war years, who are treacherous and subhuman. (In *Night People* the enemy are variously described as "the creeps over there," "burglars," "a methodical bunch of lice.") Political melodrama looks ahead.

This is the level of the anti-Communism of *Night People*. And it is at this level that the advertising-entertainment medium has political effect. In a culture which has been movie-centered for thirty years, films are a reflection of popular American thought as well as an influence upon it. At the Army-McCarthy hearings, the participants, conscious of the radio and television audience, find it necessary to proclaim, each in his turn, that he *hates* Communists. McCarthy imputes weakness and political unreliability to the Secretary of the Army by suggesting that Stevens merely *dislikes* Communists. In other words, if he knew what they were, he would *hate* them: he lacks the hero's sureness. McCarthy draws political support by the crude, yet surprisingly controlled, intensity of his hatred of Communists; the intensity suggests that he, like Intelligence Officer Peck, knows how to take care of rats, and his lack of scruples becomes a political asset. Further knowledge is irrelevant; the hero does not need to look too closely into the heart of evil.

Knowledge may even be dangerous. The hero should know that Communists are rats without needing to examine the nature of Communism. Is our thinking so primitive that we fear that a close look will not only expose us to destruction but will turn us into rats, that Communism is contagious? Is that why there is so much fear that people may read Communist literature, and why those who have had no contact with Communism are deemed the only safe anti-Communists? The man of conscience who examines the enemy sees human beings—the primitive explanation is that he got too close and was infected. If you know enough to hate Communists, you know enough; if you know more, perhaps you can no longer hate. The ritualistic nature of this popular anti-Communism was made apparent in the public reaction to Acheson's remark that he wouldn't turn his back on Alger Hiss. Acheson spoke as one human being talking about another; he was attacked for his failure to recognize that Soviet agents are not supposed to be regarded as human beings.

The morality play had meaning as an instructive dramatization, an externalization of the conflict within man. Our popular culture and popular politics and even our popular religion take this conflict and project it onto the outside world. The resulting simplification has immediate advantages: we are exonerated, they are guilty. In contrast with drama which sensitizes man to human complexity, melodrama desensitizes men. No wonder the public has no patience with real political issues, nor with the moral complexities of Shakespeare or Greek tragedy. The movies know how to do it better: in a film, Stevens or McCarthy would prove his case; in a film, Oppenheimer would be innocent or guilty. A reporter who made a telephone survey asking, "Are you listening to the Army-McCarthy hearings?" got the housewife's response: "No, that's not my idea of entertainment." It is the stereotyped heroes and villains of her brand of entertainment who react upon our public figures—so that if Stevens admitted that he had functioned in the real world of conciliation and compromise, he would be publicly dishonored (yet he cannot prove his basic honesty without making that admission).

Senator McCarthy has not the look of a man in the grip of a fixed idea; rather he has the look of a man who has the fixed idea well in hand. When national issues can be discussed in terms of "ferreting out rats" (and even McCarthy's political opponents accept the term) the man with the fixed idea is the man who appears to stand for something. He has found the role to play. When Senator McCarthy identifies himself with *right* and identifies anyone who opposes him with the Communist conspiracy, he carries the political morality play to its paranoid conclusion—a reductio ad absurdum in which right and wrong, and political good and evil, dissolve into: are you for me or against me? But the question may be asked, are not this morality and this politics fundamentally just as absurd and just as dangerous when practiced on a national scale in our commercial culture? The world is *not* divided into good and evil, enemies are *not* all alike, Communists are *not* just Nazis with a different accent; and it is precisely the task of political analysis (and the incidental function of literature and drama) to help us understand the nature of our enemies and the nature of our opposition to them. A country which accepts wars as contests between good and evil is suffering from the delusion that the morality play symbolizes real political conflicts.

Some political theorists would like to manipulate this delusion: they hold that the only way to combat Communism is to employ the "useful myth" that the current world struggle is a battle between Christianity and atheism, that the free world represents God on earth and the Communist countries, the anti-Christ. Such a "useful myth" may very likely, however, be purchased (for the most part) just as cynically as it is sold. Is a myth a myth for the public that accepts it without conviction? Or does "Fight for God" become more like the advertising slogan "Always Buy Chesterfields"—a slogan which does not prevent the Chesterfield smoker from having nagging fears of lung cancer and heart disease? The modern man who fights in a mythical holy crusade knows he's compelled to fight—whether it's for God or not.

Cecil B. DeMille, who might lay claim to having falsified history as much as any man alive, is now at work on *The Ten Commandments* (in Vista Vision). He states: "It's amazing how much our story parallels the world situation today"—the parallel may be a bit elusive, but no doubt DeMille will make his point. Other film makers, suddenly confronted with CinemaScope, have been raiding his domain; they appear to be so dazzled by the width of the screen they feel it can only be filled by God. Their primitive awe is similar to that of the public which is attracted to "big" pictures. Though it is easy to scoff at the advertising which emphasizes the *size* of a picture—the cast of thousands, the number of millions spent—magnitude in itself represents an achievement to the public. The whole family goes to *The Robe* or *The Greatest Show on Earth*—it's an event like *Gone with the Wind* or *Duel in the Sun*, as big as a natural catastrophe. Primitivism takes many forms. We no longer hear arguments on all sides about what causes wars: global atomic warfare is so big it seems to be something only God can explain. (*Night People* is not a small picture: the closing shot leaves the hero confronting the heavens.)

The danger in manipulation and cynicism is not that those who extol the greatness of the democratic idea and the greatness of the common man while treating the public as common fools are Machiavellians scheming to impose an ideology upon the public. The democratic ideology has been imposed on *them:* they are driven by economic necessity (and political necessity) to give the public what it wants. The real danger is that we may lose the capacity for those extensions in height, in depth, in space which are the experience of art and thought. If the public becomes accustomed to being pleased and pandered to, the content is drained out of democratic political life. (The pimp who peddles good clean stuff is nevertheless engaged in prostitution.)

After dozens of anti-Nazi films and countless slick stories and articles, the public had had enough of Hitler. What they wearied of had only the slenderest connection with the subject of Nazism; they got tired of the old formula with the Nazi label. But they didn't reject the formula, they settled for a change of labels. In the same way Hollywood may well exhaust anti-Communism before it has gotten near it. *Night People* is just the beginning of a new cycle—a cycle which begins by exploiting public curiosity and ends by satiating it.

All our advertising is propaganda, of course, but it has become so much a part of our life, is so pervasive, that we just don't know what it is propaganda *for*. Somehow it keeps the wheels rolling and that seems to be what it's for. Why don't other peoples see that we are the heroes and the Russians cannibals? One reason is that America's public relations romance with itself is a spectacle to the rest of the world. In Hollywood productions, the American soldiers and civilians abroad are soft touches, chivalrous under the wisecracks, patronizing and generous towards unfortunate little people the world over; aroused by injustice, the American is Robin Hood freed by birth from the threat of the Sheriff of Nottingham. Though this propaganda fails us abroad (too many Americans having been there) it functions at home as an entertaining form of self-congratulation and self-glorification: it makes the audience feel good. While we consume our own propaganda, other people are not so gullible about us. They have a different way of being gullible: the are influenced by Communist propaganda about us.

PROPAGANDA—SALT OF THE EARTH

One wonders if the hero of *Night People,* so sharp at detecting the cannibal under the Communist tunic, would recognize the Communist *position* when he saw it. *Salt of the Earth* is as clear a piece of Communist propaganda as we have had in many years, but the critic of the New York *Times* saw, ". . . in substance, simply a strong pro-labor film with a particularly sympathetic interest in the Mexican-Americans with whom it deals," and the critic of the Los Angeles *Daily News* had this to say: "If there is propaganda in this picture it is not an alien one, but an assertion of principles no thoughtful American can reject." There are Americans, then, who have not learned that Communist propaganda concentrates on local grievances. They fail to recognize that Communism makes use of principles that no thoughtful American (or Frenchman or Englishman) can reject. Communism in each region appears to be divested of its Soviet accoutrements; its aspect is not alien in Central America, South America, Europe, Asia, or Africa. It is effective because it organizes, or captures the direction of, groups struggling for status.

Despite the reactions of some critics, it is not likely that the American film audience would react favorably to the publicity campaign, "At last! An honest movie about American working people." If American working people seek an image of their attitudes and beliefs they will find it in Hollywood films—they have helped to put it there. Though a Hollywood version glamorizes their lives, it does justice to their dreams. If they did go to see *Salt* it is not likely that more than a small proportion would see anything that struck home, and that perhaps would be only as a reminder of depression days.

At special showings or at art film houses, it's a different story. *Salt* can seem true and real for those liberals and progressives whose political thinking has never gone beyond the thirties. Depression social consciousness is their exposed nerve: touch it and it becomes the only reality, more vivid than the actual conditions they live in. Many Americans felt the first stirrings of political awareness in the thirties, and nothing that has happened since has affected them comparably. They look back to the social theater and WPA art as to a Golden Age. The prosperity that followed is viewed almost as a trick, a device to conceal the truth and to prevent the oppressed workers from joining together to defeat ruthless big business. Prosperity is integrated with so much advertising and cynicism that it seems a sham—it doesn't look *real.* In search of something to believe in, they see the hollowness of the films played out in modern apartments and neat little cottages and tend to situate truth in the worst possible setting—in what has been left out of Hollywood films. What looks ugly and depressing must be true, since what looks prosperous is as empty as an ad. (The film that uses a Santa Barbara mansion for the home of its heroine doesn't advertise its documentary background, but a film using a shack, even if it is a facade, stresses truth and realism.) The depths to which they may fall have a greater emotional claim on them than the prosperity they (fearfully) enjoy. The worst makes the greatest claim to truth.

Salt of the Earth is not likely to be effective propaganda for overthrowing the capitalist bosses at home, a task which the Communists are not likely to envision in the United States anyway. But it is extremely shrewd propaganda for the urgent business of the U.S.S.R.: making colonial peoples believe that they can expect no good from the United States; convincing Europe and Asia and the rest of the world that there are no civil liberties in the U.S.A. and that our capitalism is really fascism. The American Communists are not so much interested these days in glorifying the Soviet Union as in destroying European and Asiatic faith in the United States. Fifteen years ago it would have been easy to toss off a film like *Salt* with "it's worse than propaganda, it's a dull movie." Flippancy makes us rather uneasy today: Communist propaganda, seizing upon our failures and our imperfections, and, when these are not strong enough, inventing others, has very nearly succeeded in discrediting us to the whole world. The discreditable aspects of American life are realities to be dealt with. Communist propaganda, however, treats them as opportunities.

The raw material of *Salt of the Earth* is a 1951–1952 strike of Mexican-American zinc miners in New Mexico. The film, made in 1953, was sponsored by the International Union of Mine, Mill and Smelter Workers (expelled from the CIO in 1950 as Communist-dominated), and financed by Independent Productions Corporation (the money was "borrowed from liberal Americans"). The writer, director, and producer are blacklisted in Hollywood as fellow travelers.

What brought these people together to make a film—zinc miners, liberal Americans, blacklisted film makers? This was no mere commercial enterprise, and in our brief history as a nation of film addicts, there has never been anything like a group of several hundred people working together in devotion to film art. If art was their aim, how misguided their effort—for what work of art, in any field, has ever resulted from "group discussion and collective constructive criticism" ("no less than 400 people had read, or heard a reading of, the screenplay by the time we commenced production"). Collective constructive criticism—where have we heard that term before? It is not irony but justice that the artists who chose this method came out with a film as dreary and programmatic as the films made by those who have collective criticism forced upon them.

Here is the opening of the film and our introduction to the heroine, Esperanza: "A woman at work chopping wood. Though her back is to the camera, we sense her weariness in toil by the set of her shoulders . . . we begin to gather that she is large with child. The woman carries the load of wood to an outdoor fire, staggering under its weight. . . ." It doesn't take us long to find out that this is eternal downtrodden woman, but if we're slow, her first words set us straight: "How shall I begin my story that has no beginning? How shall I start the telling of all that is yet becoming?"

The miners of *Salt of the Earth* are striking for equality (principally equality of safety conditions) with the "Anglos," but the strike is not a bargaining weapon for definite limited objectives. It is inflated with lessons, suggestions and implications until it acquires symbolic status. This is the dialogue as the hero Ramon watches Esperanza, his wife, nursing the baby:

> *Ramon:* A fighter, huh?
> *Esperanza:* He was born fighting. And born hungry.
> *Ramon:* Drink, drink, Juanito. You'll never have it so good.
> *Esperanza:* He'll have it good. Some day.
> *Ramon* (half-whispering): Not just Juanito. You'll have it good too, Esperanza. We're going to win this strike.
> *Esperanza:* What makes you so sure?
> *Ramon* (brooding): Because if we lose, we lose more than a strike. We lose the union. And the men know this. And if we win, we win more than a few demands. We win . . . (groping for words) something bigger. Hope. Hope for our kids. Juanito can't grow strong on milk alone.

This is a strike in which the workers *grow*. "Have you learned nothing from this strike?" Esperanza asks her husband, and speaks of her own development: "I want to rise. And push everything up with me as I go. . . ." "Strike" in *Salt of the Earth* is used in its revolutionary meaning, as a training ground in solidarity, a preparation for the big strike to come—a microcosm of the coming revolution.

If the author had cut up a pamphlet and passed out the parts, he wouldn't have given out anything very different from this:

> *Esperanza:* They tried to turn people against us. They printed lies about us in their newspapers. . . . They said . . . that all the Mexicans ought to be sent back where they came from. But the men said . . .
> *Antonio* (slapping newspaper): How can I go back where I came from. The shack I was born in is buried under company property.
> *Kalinsky:* Why don't nobody ever tell the bosses to go back where they came from?
> *'Cente:* Wouldn't be no bosses in the state of New Mexico if they did.
> *Alfredo* (dreamily): Brother! Live to see the day!
> *Antonio:* Talk about wide open spaces! Far as the eye can see—no Anglos.

Ramon holds up a finger, correcting him.

Ramon: No Anglo *bosses.*

This pedagogical tone, so reminiscent of the thirties, is maintained throughout much of the film. Social realism has never been able to pass up an opportunity for instruction: these strikers are always teaching each other little constructive lessons. Here is Ramon reprimanding Frank, the "Anglo" union organizer, for his failure to recognize a picture of Juarez:

> *Ramon:* . . . If I didn't know a picture of George Washington, you'd say I was an awful dumb Mexican.
> *Frank* (deeply chagrined): I'm an awful dumb Anglo . . . I've got a lot to learn.

Then, of course, there are the big lessons: when Esperanza is in labor and the Sheriff is asked to get the doctor he responds with, "You kiddin'? Company doctor won't come to no picket line." A miner's widow then speaks to the men picketing: "They, up there, your bosses—they don't care whether your children live or die. Let them be born like animals! (A pause.) Remember this while you're marching, you men. Remember well." (She spits in the road.)

Another facet of social realism is the inflation of dialogue to the rank of folk wisdom (*Ramon:* " 'No money down. Easy term payments.' I tell you something: this installment plan, it's the curse of the working class.") and folk wit (*Esperanza:* "Finding scabs in Zinc town, Ramon said, was like looking for a rich man in heaven . . ."). These "oppressed" are not confused by book-learning and bosses' lies. They are the custodians of the real social truth.

The story is not just slanted: the slant *is* the story. Even the baby's christening party—in the nighttime—is interrupted by deputy sheriffs with a repossession order for the radio. When the company gets an eviction order, we see the deputies "dumping the precious accumulations of a lifetime on to the road: the shrine, a kewpie doll, a faded photograph." And, of course, the photograph of Juarez is "smashed in the dust." If you have half an eye for this sort of thing, you'll know when you first see Esperanza's shiny radio that it will be taken away from her, just as you'll know when you see the photograph of Juarez that it wouldn't be framed except to be smashed.

Detail upon detail adds up to a picture of fascism. How can responsible critics fail to see what they're getting? Well, something has been added to this old popular front morality play, something that seems to give it new credibility.

The superintendent of the mine (from his Cadillac) suggests to the sheriff that it would be nice to cut Ramon "down to size." The sheriff "touches his Stetson courteously" and, a few moments later, gives the signal to four deputies—Vance, Kimbrough and two others. They arrest Ramon (who offers no resistance), handcuff him and thrust him into their car. Vance, "a pale, cavernous, slackjawed man," is "slowly drawing on a pigskin glove." After an exchange of a few words, the "gloved hand comes up, swipes Ramon across his mouth," as Vance says softly, "Now you know that ain't no way to talk to a white man."

Ramon sits tense now, awaiting the next blow. A trickle of blood runs down his chin. The two deputies in front sit like wax dummies, paying no attention to what is going on in back.

Kimbrough: Hey, Vance. You said this Mex was full of pepper. He don't look so peppery now.

Vance: Oh, but he is. This bullfighter's full of chile.

He drives a gloved fist into Ramon's belly. Ramon gasps, his eyes bulge. . . . Vance strikes him in the abdomen again. Kimbrough snickers. . . . Ramon is doubled up, his head between his legs. Vance pulls him erect.

Vance: Hold your head up, Pancho. That ain't no way to sit.

Ramon (a mutter in Spanish): I'll outlive you all, you lice.

Vance (softly): How's that? What's that Spic talk?

He strikes Ramon in the belly. Ramon gives a choked cry. . . . Kimbrough holds up Ramon's head while Vance punches him methodically. Ramon gasps in Spanish:

Ramon: Mother of God . . . have mercy. . . .

As if this were not enough, the next shots of Ramon being struck in the belly are intercut with Esperanza's contractions as she gives birth. Finally, "the two images merge, and undulate, and blur . . . we hear the feeble wail of a newborn infant."

This full dress racial treatment is the politically significant ingredient in *Salt of the Earth.* Although socially, economically and legally the United States has been expiating its sins against minorities in record time, it is still vulnerable. The Communists exploit this vulnerability: the message for export is that America is a fascist country which brutally oppresses the darker peoples.

Frank, *Salt*'s union organizer, tells us that "equality's the one thing the bosses can't afford." The explanation offered is pitifully inadequate: "The biggest club they have over the Anglo locals is, 'well—at least you get more than the Mexicans.' " Ramon replies, "Okay, so discrimination hurts the Anglo too, but it hurts me more. And I've had enough of it." This catechism of Communist economics has a creaky sound. A rational Ramon in a film set in 1951 might very well ask: Why can't this company afford equality when so many others can?

To ask that would expose the mystification central to *Salt of the Earth* by indicating that this community is no microcosm of our society, and that the situation depicted is grotesquely far from typical. The film's strike has not been placed against the background of American life which would provide perspective and contrast. It stays within a carefully composed system of references. (Esperanza describes the help the striking miners got—"messages of solidarity and the crumpled dollar bills of working men." After fifteen years of wanting to know who the company president is, the miners come across a picture of him in a

"Man of Distinction" ad. One of the men in the union truck that delivers food to the starving miners is a Negro; when a miner comes over, "the Negro leans down and shakes his hand warmly.")

Let's take a look at the film's claims to truth and "honesty." The union president (who played Ramon) has written that a Production Committee had "the responsibility of seeing that our picture ran true to life from start to finish. Occasionally there were meetings in which the union people pointed out to our Hollywood friends that a scene we had just shot was not true in certain details. When that happened, we all pitched in to correct the mistake." I think we may accept the evidence that those several hundred people who made the film believed that it was *true;* from this it does not follow, however, that we can assume that all the film's incidents belong to the period of the 1951–1952 strike.

Let's take a further look at what the union president writes: "We don't have separate pay rates any more. . . . Thank God for our union and for the men who organized it. Back in the 'thirties, they were blacklisted, thrown off company property and told to take their houses with them . . . *Salt of the Earth* was not intended to be a documentary record of that particular strike (1951–1952). But I will say this. It is a true account of our people's lives and struggles." So perhaps the eviction in the film does not derive from the 1951–1952 strike; perhaps the miners in 1951–1952 were not striking for equal safety conditions at all. And it would still be a "true," honest movie to those who made it. If they accept this film as "fundamentally" true of their lives, a "symbolic" truth that is higher, *more* true than the plain details of that strike, then, probably, they can also take the next step, and believe that their struggle is typical and symbolic of American society (the sheriff who takes orders and bribes from the bosses symbolizes government as capitalism's hired man; the company officers represent the decadent quality of American business; the love story of Ramon and Esperanza symbolizes the vitality of the masses, etc.).

Can the people who had a "constructive" hand in the script believe in the abstract, symbolic characters as representations of their lives? Don't the miners' wives see that something is wrong somewhere when the famous Mexican actress who plays Esperanza, the symbol of *their* lives, is so unlike them? The miners' wives—big women in slacks and jackets, with short permanented hair, and a pleasant, rather coarse plainness—suggest the active, liberated manner of free American women. Esperanza, fine-boned, gentle and passive, her long hair pulled back, dressed in drab, long skirts, is the Madonna on the picket line. Can the women accept nobility incarnate as the image of themselves? Or is it that they have gotten so far into symbolic thinking that they believe in this heroine not merely as their representative but as the symbol of all suffering humanity ("Esperanza" means "hope")—so that she doesn't really have to be at all like them, since she represents a higher truth about them? I think we must allow for the possibility that those who see themselves as symbols are capable also of holding rather symbolic notions of truth.

Just for fun, let's try out *Salt*'s realistic method. We decide that a true account of Negro life in a Northern city begs to be done. We take the simple story of a Negro girl led into a life of vice and crime by a white business man who seduces her and then casts her off on his corrupt cronies. We follow her to the brothel where she is forced to work (our brothel scenes are the first authentic record of a brothel to be included in a work of art). We take incidents from actual newspaper stories (the police own the brothel; city big-shots cover-up for the police). Real prostitutes not only play themselves, they supply us with information that makes it possible for us to give accurate representations of the impotent and perverted white businessmen who are their clients. The girls are rather a buxom crew, but our heroine (we were fortunate indeed to secure the services of Miss Greer Garson, who had dreamed all her life of playing a noble Negro prostitute)[1] suggests endurance and infinite patience. The heroine's only friends are among the other prostitutes—and, as there is a white girl among them, she learns that not all white people are customers: there are white workers, too. The brutal mechanization of the heroine's existence is forcefully presented in a sequence intercutting from her room to the rooms of the other girls. When, finally, the girls realize that in solidarity there is strength, they force the white madam (a cold, shrewd, hard-eyed aristocrat) to grant them better percentages.

Have we told any lies? There is nothing in it that hasn't happened at some time. All we had to do was select the data carefully and build up the story so that no "extraneous" material showing other forms of Negro life entered in. And it would be simple enough to inflate the dialogue so that the brothel becomes a microcosm of America, a symbol of race relations under fascism. Perhaps the best way to expose the falsification is to point out the brothel down the street—with white workers and a Negro clientele, and hence to suggest that perhaps America is too vast and pluralistic an enterprise to be symbolized in any one brothel.

If we want to know something about the treatment of minority peoples in the United States we don't look at one community, we examine and compare data in various communities, cities, industries and institutions. We examine the extraordinary social phenomenon of pecking (in one town the Irish peck the Italians, in the next the Italians peck the Mexicans, in other towns the Mexicans peck the Negroes, and some cities are a regular chicken yard, with Armenians or Portuguese last in the line) and other forms of internecine warfare among minorities. We look at the life of the integrated as well as the unintegrated minorities; we don't assume that the life of the Mexican-American zinc miner is more symbolic of the treatment of minorities than the life of the corner grocer whose name is Ramirez.

---

1. Miss Rosaura Revueltas (Esperanza): "In a way it seemed I had waited all my life to be in this picture. My own mother was a miner's daughter."

Compare *Salt of the Earth* with the films—*social* films, too—of artists whose work is informed with individual imagination. Buñuel, whose shocking *Los Olvidados* gives the lie to the concept that the oppressed are the salt of the earth. De Sica, whose joyful little masterpiece *Miracle in Milan* flouted the expectations of Americans who looked to Italian neo-realism for sombre, serious "truth." Eisenstein, who selected and stacked his images for ideological purposes, but who did it, at least, on a grand scale. The enemy was flamboyantly gross and evil, the violence obsessively brutal. Barbaric splendor, excesses overflowed the bounds of the ideology—just as Griffith's fairy tale riches could not be contained in the moralistic framework of *Intolerance*. These artists use the film as a feast for eye and mind.

The proletarian morality play is a strict form: the heroes and villains illustrate a lesson. The hero is humanity, the struggling worker trying to reach consciousness of his historical role. He is vital, full of untapped strength; the brutal oppression to which he has been subjected has made him all the more human.[2] He is a man who can learn. The villains are the hero's class enemies— they are representatives of a decadent ruling class and they must be taught a lesson. Though they control economic power, they are personally weak: they have lost the life-force. They are subhuman. The play is not so much a sermon as a guide to action. It serves as a demonstration of the potential strength of the working class—or, in this case, minority peoples. *Salt of the Earth* is full of violence; it avails itself of the excitations of melodrama, but the violence is symbolic.

Communists have their own fear of infection: the member or sympathizer who explores other ideas may be deflected from orthodoxy; he may succumb to the attractions of "bourgeois" thought. Unless he stays within the bounds of the approved ideas, he jeopardizes his own dedication to the cause and he may infect the circle of his acquaintances.

"Social realism" is supposed to derive its art from reality. The art is negligible and nothing could be further from reality than these abstractions performing symbolic actions in a depressing setting. The setting does refer to the real world, however, and *Salt of the Earth* can seem "true" to people who have been in the Imperial Valley or New Mexico or the southern states. They have seen shocking living conditions and they may feel the moral necessity to do something about them. Communist propaganda takes this desire and converts it into a sense of anxiety and distress by "demonstrating" that all of American power supports this shocking situation and thus uses this situation for a total

---

2. The glorification of the common man denies him his humanity in the very process of setting him up as more human than others. If you believe in the greatness of the oppressed, you are very likely not looking at the oppressed at all, but at an image of what they should be. Marx predicted that a degenerate society would degrade the working class; the latter day "Marxists" accept the notion of a degenerate society but hold as a concomitant the curious notion of an uncontaminated "oppressed." The concept is not analytic, of course, but propagandistic.

condemnation of American life. The moral sensibility that has given vitality to American principles is manipulated by these propagandists into a denial that America stands for those principles, and into an insistence that the *real* principles of American life are revealed in the sore spot. The moral person feels helpless and alienated unless he accepts the path that is offered to him—identifying his moral interests with the revolutionary aims of the working class.

It is symptomatic of the dangers in a commercialized culture that these people—the ones who made the film and the ones who believe it—can find nothing else in American life to which they can give allegiance. They are articulate, literate. They are, no doubt, sincere in their dedication to the cause of the downtrodden. A film like *Salt of the Earth* seems so ridiculously and patently false that it requires something like determination to consider that those who make it believe in it. They serve a higher truth—and, of course, they have a guiding thread for their beliefs, a lifeline which directs them through the maze of realities and symbols. Those who hold the other end of the line are very shrewd in jerking it—now this way, now that. But what artist with vision or imagination could keep his fist closed so tight?

FOR DISCUSSION

1.   The section on American "Cold War" propaganda films indicates that movies in this category, unlike the World War II products on which they were modeled, were mostly box-office failures. How can this be explained? Is it indicative that the whole style of American movie propaganda is severely dated? Noting the failure of this kind of cinematic mass persuasion, what other directions are open to film as a propaganda medium? To what extent does national mood condition the effectiveness of propaganda?

2.   Why do you suppose that Pauline Kael titled her piece "Morality Plays Right and Left"? What does she mean by "morality plays"? Why does she label *Night People* as *advertising* and *Salt of the Earth* as *propaganda?* What's the difference, if any, between the terms as she is using them here?

3.   Summarize the arguments Ms. Kael uses in denouncing films like *Night People* and *Salt of the Earth.* Whether or not you screen either of the pictures, you have seen dozens like them, where the good guys always give it to the bad guys (what else is on TV?), or where exploited people triumph over their exploiters in another version of the good guy-bad guy morality play. Do you think Ms. Kael is overreacting to what is either harmless entertainment (in *Night People*) or necessary morale-building (in *Salt of the Earth*)? Or do you agree with her stated or implied convictions that there are serious dangers to the health of a society that indulges itself in such cynical and naïve simple-mindedness? Discuss.

Filmography

Filmography

"CLASSIC" PROPAGANDA FILMS

Potemkin. 86 minutes. Silent. Directed by Sergei M. Eisenstein, 1925. Rental from Audio-Brandon Films.

Triumph of the Will. 120 minutes. Black and White. Directed by Leni Riefenstahl, 1934. Rental from Museum of Modern Art (without subtitles), Contemporary-McGraw-Hill Films (with English subtitles), or Audio-Brandon Films (with English subtitles). The Museum of Modern Art has an abbreviated 40-minute version with subtitles at a low rental. This version should be sufficient for high school classes.

AMERICAN WAR PROPAGANDA FILMS

Hearts of the World. 180 minutes. Silent. Black and White. Directed by D. W. Griffith, 1918. Rental from Audio-Brandon Films.

Confessions of a Nazi Spy. 102 minutes. Black and White. Directed by Anatole Litvak, 1939. Rental from United Artists 16.

The Ramparts We Watch. 60 minutes. Black and White. Directed by Louis de Rochemont (*March of Time* series), 1940. Rental from Audio-Brandon Films.

The Mortal Storm. 110 minutes. Black and White. Directed by Frank Borzage, 1940. Rental from Films Inc.

The Great Dictator. 115 minutes. Black and White. Directed by Charles Chaplin, 1940. Rental from RBC Films.

Wake Island. 78 minutes. Black and White. Directed by John Farrow, 1942. Rental from Universal 16.

Bataan. 114 minutes. Black and White. Directed by Tay Garnett, 1943. Rental from Films Inc.

Lifeboat. 97 minutes. Black and White. Directed by Alfred Hitchcock, 1944. Rental from Audio-Brandon Films.

Why We Fight. Documentary series produced by Frank Capra. Films run in length from 42 minutes to 80 minutes: *Prelude to War, The Nazis Strike, Divide and Conquer, Battle of Britain, Battle of Russia, Battle of China, War Comes to America.* Rental from Twyman Films.

Mission to Moscow. 123 minutes. Black and White. Directed by Michael Curtiz, 1943. Rental from United Artists 16.

THE COLD WAR

I Was a Communist for the FBI. 83 minutes. Black and White. Directed by Gordon Douglas, 1951. Check local film sources for rental.

My Son John. 122 minutes. Black and White. Directed by Leo McCarey, 1952. Check local film sources for rental.

Night People. 93 minutes. Color. Directed by Nunnally Johnson, 1954. Rental from Films Inc.

Salt of the Earth. 94 minutes. Black and White. Directed by Herbert Biberman, 1954. Rental from Audio-Brandon Films.

SELECTED 16 MM FILM RENTAL LIBRARIES

Audio-Brandon Films. 34 MacQuesten Parkway So., Mount Vernon, N. Y. 10550. Tel.: (914) 664-5051. *Branches:* 2138 East 7th St., Chicago, Ill. 60649. Tel.: (312) MU 4-2531. 406 Clement St., San Francisco, Calif. 94118. Tel.: (415) SK 2-4800.

Contemporary-McGraw-Hill Films. 230 West 42nd St., New York, N. Y. Tel.: (212) 971-3333. *Eastern Office:* Princeton Road, Highstown, N. J. 08520. Tel.: (609) 448-1700. *Midwest Office:* 828 Custer Ave., Evanston, Ill. 60202. Tel.: (312) 869-5010. *Western Office:* 1714 Stockton St., San Francisco, Calif. 94133. Tel.: (415) 362-3115.

Films Inc.—9 offices, regionally. 1) 227 Pharr Road, N. E., Atlanta, Ga. 30305. Tel.: (404) 237-0341. (Georgia, Alabama, Florida, Mississippi, North and South Carolina, and Tennessee.) 2) 161 Massachusetts Ave., Boston, Mass. 02115. Tel.: (617) 937-1110. (Massachusetts, Connecticut, Maine, New Hampshire, Rhode Island, and Vermont.) 3) 1414 Dragon St., Dallas, Tex. 75207. Tel.: (214) 741-4071. (Texas, Arkansas, Louisiana, New Mexico, and Oklahoma.) 4) 5625 Hollywood Blvd., Hollywood, Calif. 90028. Tel:. (213) 466-5481. (California, Arizona, Colorado, Nevada, Utah, and Wyoming.) 5) 3501 Queens Blvd., Long Island City, N. Y. Tel.: (212) 937-1110. (New York, New Jersey, Delaware, Maryland, Pennsylvania, Virginia, and Washington, D. C.) 6) 2129 N. E. Broadway, Portland, Oreg. 97232. Tel.: (503) 282-5558. (Oregon, Idaho, Montana, and Washington.) 7) 44 East South Temple, Salt Lake City, Utah. Tel.: (801) 328-8191. (Utah and Idaho.) 8) 3034 Canon St. (Kerr Film Exchange), San Diego, Calif. Tel.: (714) 224-2406. (San Diego Metropolitan Area) 9) 4420 Oakton St., Skokie, Ill. 60076. Tel.: (312) 676-1088 (Skokie), (312) 583-3330 (Chicago). (Illinois, Indiana, Iowa, Kansas, Kentucky, Michigan, Minnesota, Missouri, Nebraska, North and South Dakota, West Virginia, and Ohio.)

Museum of Modern Art, Department of Film Circulating Programs. 11 West 53rd St., New York, N. Y. 10022. Tel.: (212) 245-8900.

RBC Films. 933 No. La Brea Ave., Los Angeles, Calif., 90038.

Twyman Films. 329 Salem Ave., Dayton, Ohio 45401. Tel.: (513) 222-4014.
United Artists 16. 729 Seventh Ave., New York, N. Y. 10019. Tel.: (212) 245-6000.
Universal 16. 221 Park Ave. So., New York, N. Y. 10003. Tel.: (212) 777-6600.